Contents

How to Use This Workbook

Welcome to the *Progress over Perfection Workbook*, where you'll find the tools you need to begin creating essential productivity habits that will help you make enormous progress without burning out. This workbook is a companion to the book *Progress over Perfection*, where you can learn more about how to break out of the shackles of perfectionism, set boundaries in your life, create productivity habits that work for you, and still achieve your biggest goals.

The exercises you'll find inside this workbook will help you quickly see meaningful changes in your own life. You'll soon find that you start to feel less stressed and frazzled, and more intentional in the way you live and work. Oh, and here's the crazy thing. Not only will you feel less anxious and overwhelmed, but you'll also be way more productive! A study by the health

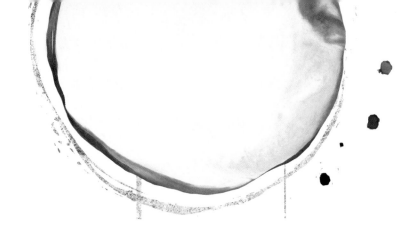

insurance company Aetna found that by incorporating healthier productivity habits, employees added an extra 60 minutes of productivity into their week.

This workbook will also help you embrace mindfulness by helping you stay present. As you put pen to paper, it encourages you to tune into what you're thinking and feeling—rather than getting distracted by your smartphone, or thoughts about what to cook for dinner. After all, at the heart of mindfulness is the idea of bringing your attention to the present moment, rather than ruminating on the past or fretting about the future. It's about observing your experience in its entirety—any thoughts, feelings, and body sensations—rather than policing yourself.

By bringing a mindful approach to productivity, we can tune out what our so-called "competitors" are doing and focus on what we need to do to move forward. And by embracing the fact that we can do anything, not everything, we can start taking imperfect-yet-meaningful steps toward our biggest goals.

Whether you're a CEO, a working mama, a side-hustlin' babe, or an entrepreneur, we're all on this quest together. Let's do this!

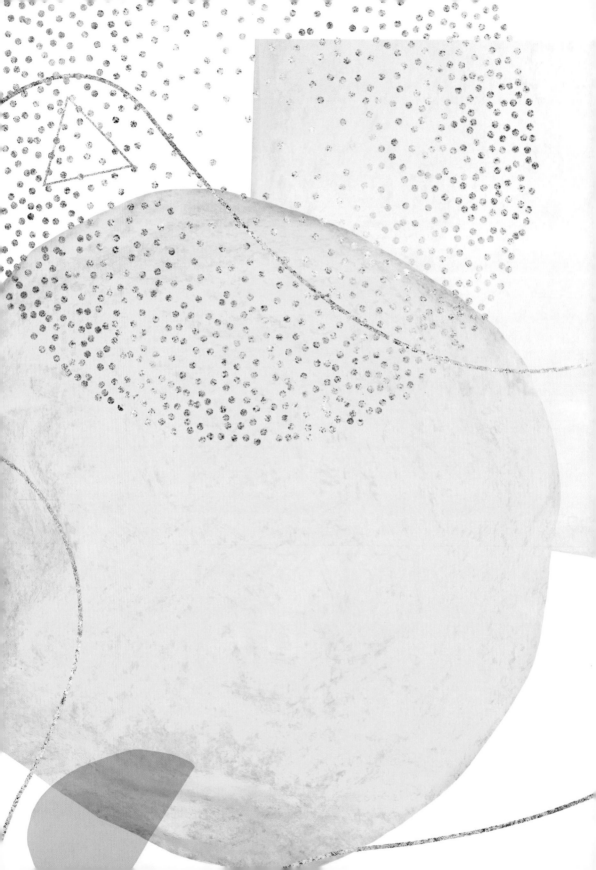

Overcoming Perfection Paralysis

For many high achievers, being a "perfectionist" is worn like a badge of honor. Like being busy or stressed, it tends to go hand in hand with the idea of being a hard worker. But while holding yourself to an impossibly high standard may seem impressive or honorable, it can actually hold you back in life. Why? Because "perfection" simply doesn't exist! You wouldn't continue climbing a mountain if you knew there was no summit, right? That would be freakin' exhausting and pointless. Well, relentlessly pursuing perfection is pretty much the same thing.

The Perfection Myth

When you set impossible standards for yourself, it does you more harm than good. First, you set yourself up for failure. So, even when you do make some amazing progress toward your goals, you're still left feeling like it's never enough. Instead of acknowledging the fact that you're stronger and fitter and wiser than the woman you were yesterday, you're begrudging the fact that you're still not as strong or fit or talented as that woman you see on your Instagram feed. Second, it can be seriously detrimental to your well-being—both physically and mentally. Just like scaling that never-ending mountain, constantly chasing perfection is going to run you ragged. The result is that you'll be too exhausted and depleted to enjoy all the amazingness you already have right in front of you!

You may be thinking, "But what do you mean there's no such thing as perfection, Emma?! Have you not seen that YouTube video of Tom Hardy with cute puppies, or eaten ramen on a cold, rainy day?" Yes, these things are undeniably glorious, but they still don't equal perfection. Nor do those models you see on your Instagram feed, or that "competitor" in your industry who seems like she can do no wrong. And that's because the idea of perfection is incredibly subjective.

One person's idea of "perfection" can be someone else's "please get that thing away from me immediately." Think of it like cooking: you can have a delicious dish cooked to perfection, but there are still going to be people who don't like that particular food. The point is, unless you happen to be a piece of poultry with a thermometer in your butt, there's no universal authority to tell you when you've reached "perfect." So, let's all let go of the idea that it's something we should be striving for.

Five People You Love

Make a list of the five people you value most in your life. Then, write down what you love about them. Chances are, you don't love them because they're "perfect," but rather because of the little idiosyncrasies that make them who they are. Next, practice showing yourself that same compassion!

Person 1:

What I love about this person:

Person 2:

What I love about this person:

Person 3:

What I love about this person:

Person 4:

What I love about this person:

Person 5:

What I love about this person:

Growing From Mistakes

If you never make mistakes in life or experience rejection, then chances are you're not venturing far outside your comfort zone or taking enough risks. Try this exercise to practice adopting a "growth" mindset—when you believe that you learn and grow from your mistakes, rather than letting them make you feel "less than." Next time you make what you deem a mistake, jot down three things you can learn from it. This can help you face failure head-on!

My mistake:

Things I learned from it:

1.

2.

3.

How can I use this to progress in the future?

My mistake:

Things I learned from it:

1.

2.

3.

✳ How can I use this to progress in the future?

Visualize Your Goal

If you want to succeed at reaching a goal, it's so important to be able to imagine what success would look like. Find a quiet spot, close your eyes, and visualize what it would feel like to achieve one of your goals. Really take the time to envision the finer details and the sensations you would experience. For example, perhaps your goal is wearing a bikini to the beach for the first time and not feeling self-conscious about your body. Imagine the sound of the lapping waves, the sand crunching between your toes, the warm sun on your skin. Transporting yourself into that moment can help you tap into a positive mind-set to achieve your goals. After you practice this visualization exercise, ask yourself the following questions.

What did I hear?

What did I see?

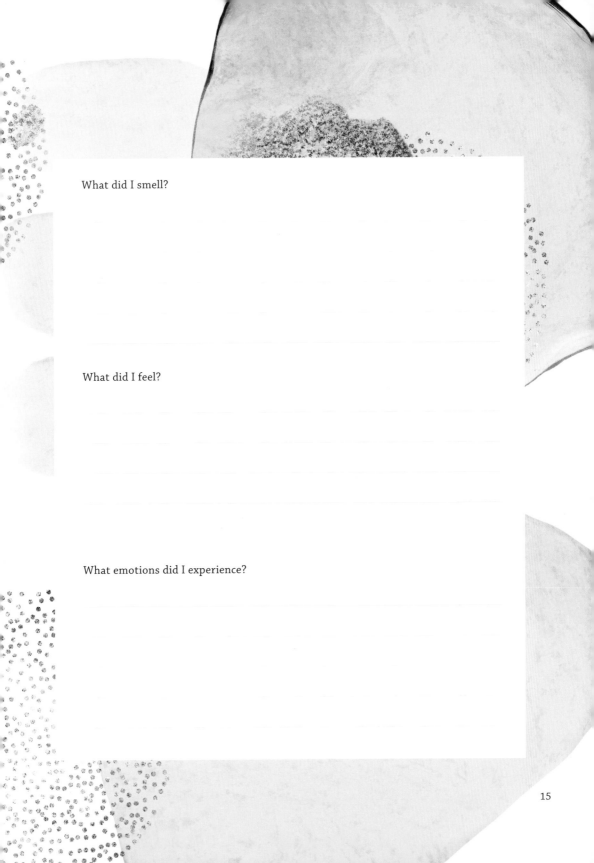

What did I smell?

What did I feel?

What emotions did I experience?

Take the First Step

Do one thing today that moves you closer to the goal you visualized on page 14. It doesn't have to be huge—it could be buying the domain name for your website or booking a tour of that weight-lifting gym. Taking that small first step will help build the momentum that will keep you moving in the right direction.

What is my goal?

What small step can I take today to move closer to that goal?

How did it feel to take that step?

_____

_____

_____

_____

_____

_____

_____

What could be a good next step?

_____

_____

_____

_____

_____

_____

_____

_____

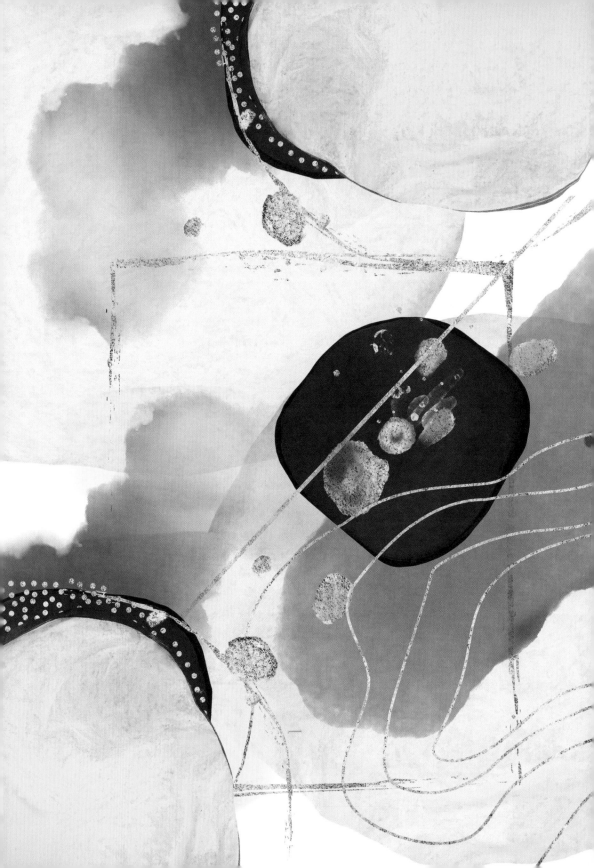

Setting Goals That Stick

I'm a firm believer in setting big, lofty, and kind of crazy goals for yourself. They give you something to work toward—actionable steps to get you closer to living your best, most fulfilling life. They help fuel your motivation and give you a sense of direction. Plus, there's nothing quite like checking a goal off your list with a big, satisfying tick! But much like cups of coffee or shades of lipstick, not all goals are created equal. If you don't have a strong, burning "why" behind your ambitions, they can set you up for (perceived) failure and disappointment.

Set Better Goals for Yourself

Many of us have experienced the goal black hole—where they disappear into oblivion—usually at the beginning of a new year. Often, we feel pressured to write down a bunch of New Year's resolutions (in a fresh diary, of course, because that's the most exciting part). We jot down goals we think we should be striving for—say, lose ten pounds, or save for a house—because that's what everyone else is doing. But by the time March or even February rolls around, we've already completely neglected our objectives.

"What is wrong with me?" you might ask yourself with exasperation while staring at your double-digit bank balance or the collection of empty candy wrappers that surround you. I'm here to tell you there's absolutely nothing wrong with you, but there is something wrong with your goals.

The good news is, you don't have to give up on setting goals completely. It's all about making your goals work for you, not the other way around. Here are some actionable tips for setting—and sticking to—your goals.

Your goals should light you up inside like a Christmas tree and make you feel excited about all the possibilities your future holds. They shouldn't necessarily make you feel comfortable—after all, greatness is rarely achieved from your comfort zone—that is, unless you're on the couch working on your side hustle in your sweats. In which case, you do you, girl!

Your dreams should scare you a little—but it should feel more like the exhilaration you get on a rollercoaster or while doing public speaking than a slow, insidious sense of dread. Your goals shouldn't make you want to hibernate under your duvet and wonder how many times in a week you can give the "Oh no, I think I'm coming down with something" excuse. And if they do? It's time to say "sayonara" to those goals and create new ones. Because at the end of the day, your goals need to fit you perfectly, like your favorite pair of jeans.

Your Big Picture

When it comes to setting better goals, the first step is making sure they align with your big-picture vision for your life. In this exercise, you'll work on visualizing exactly what that is.

What do I want my life to look like in a year's time?

_____

_____

_____

_____

_____

_____

_____

What do I want my life to look like in five years?

_____

_____

_____

_____

_____

_____

_____

_____

What do I want my life to look like in ten years?

What would I be doing with my life if I knew I couldn't fail?

What would I be doing if I had infinite time and money?

What are some of the obstacles between me and achieving these goals?

What are some small, concrete steps I could take now to get closer to those goals, or to remove some of those obstacles?

Real-life Example

Find a real-life example of someone who has achieved that big goal you want to achieve—whether it's becoming a professional ballet dancer or opening your own restaurant. Then, work backward to figure out the steps you need to take to get there. If you're feeling extra confident, you could also approach them for mentoring. Remember, fortune favors the bold!

Who is my real-life example?

What have they achieved that I also want to achieve? In what time frame do I want to achieve this goal?

What steps did this person take to get where they are today?

What obstacles did this person overcome, and how did they do this?

What steps would I need to take to get to the same place?

Three Actionable Steps

Let's say in five years you see yourself entering a different career path. Rather than becoming overwhelmed by the enormity of it, think about three smaller, actionable steps you can take now that can set you up for that bigger goal.

Research your desired career path and what skills are needed to follow that path. What transferrable skills do you already have that you can you use to transition over? What skills do you still need to develop and how can you develop those skills within your current time frame?

Network with people who are currently in that field, whether it's online or in person at industry events. Where are some places you might be able to meet others in that field? What would you hope to learn from them?

Apply for an entry-level position to get started, or perhaps apply for a part-time role or an internship. Or in your spare time, volunteer at an organization that relates to that career. Brainstorm ideas here for where you might be able to apply or volunteer:

Break It Down

By having a set time frame in which you aim to achieve your goals, you can ensure you're constantly making progress toward them—even if it's slow and steady. You'll want to break your goal into quarterly, monthly, weekly, and daily chunks. Write actionable steps toward your goal for each time frame in the boxes below.

At the beginning of the quarter:

Monthly:

Weekly:

Daily:

At the beginning of the quarter:

Monthly:

Weekly:

Daily:

At the beginning of the quarter:

Monthly:

Weekly:

Daily:

At the beginning of the quarter:

Monthly:

Weekly:

Daily:

Rate Your Readiness

Write down all the skills, attributes, and resources you would need to have in order to achieve your goal, and rate yourself on each one from one to ten. So, let's say you want to play your first live show as a musician. You would need technical proficiency to play your instrument, confidence onstage, familiarity with the songs to play them by heart, some marketing know-how to get the word out, and so forth. You could even enlist a (very honest) friend or family member to rate you on your skills in these categories. Of course, we're all about getting out into the world before you're 100 percent ready, but this can help to give you some concrete steps to work toward.

Skills, Attributes, and Resources   Rating

Skills, Attributes, and Resources   Rating

Make Micro-Progress

Think about the smallest possible task you could do to make micro-progress toward your goals. This should be something that takes you only a moment to do. For example, if you're writing a business plan, it could be writing a sentence a day. Or, if you want to spring-clean your home, it could be dusting or tidying one surface a day. If you want to save money, you could even set a round-up feature on a banking app so that you don't even notice the money coming out of your bank account. Then, make a commitment to do these micro-tasks each and every day. Below, you'll find a space where you can write out three micro-goals and check off your progress on each over the course of a week. Then at the end, you can reflect on how you did with your goals this week.

Micro-goal #1:

Monday	Tuesday	Wednesday	Thursday	Friday	Saturday	Sunday

Micro-goal #2:

Monday	Tuesday	Wednesday	Thursday	Friday	Saturday	Sunday

Micro-goal #3:

Monday	Tuesday	Wednesday	Thursday	Friday	Saturday	Sunday

How did it go this week? Did you make progress on your micro-goals? How did it feel?

Better Goals Cheat Sheet

Sick of constantly setting goals, only for them to completely fall by the wayside within a couple of months, weeks, or even days? By asking yourself these questions, you can set goals you'll actually stick to and achieve!

My goal:

Why do I want to achieve this goal?

Is this goal realistic for me? What would need to change to make it realistic?

In what time frame do I want to achieve this goal?

How will I track my progress toward this goal?

How will I celebrate if I achieve this goal?

Celebrate Good Times

Here's the fun part! Designate some rewards for when you tick off your progress goals—both big and small. Now, this doesn't mean treating yourself to the point that it detracts from your progress. For example, it would be kind of counterintuitive to spend $100 on a pair of shoes every time you reach your monthly goal of saving $500! But, you could treat yourself to a $10 face mask to pamper yourself at home instead. It doesn't have to be extravagant; it's simply about taking the time to do something that makes you feel good. Much like giving your fur baby a treat, it's kind of like a form of positive reinforcement for yourself!

What are some ways I could celebrate achieving a step toward my goal?

Once you've decided how you're going to celebrate, this can form the basis of a visualization exercise. It can be helpful to envision yourself celebrating once you achieve your goal—especially when things feel challenging. The bigger your goal is, the bigger your celebration can be. For instance, if you're writing a book and are lacking motivation to get some writing done, imagine yourself having a book launch party with friends and family in a beautiful café. Having that light at the end of the tunnel is incredibly helpful!

What did I imagine when I visualized my celebration or result? What could I see, hear, smell, and touch?

How did I feel when I imagined reaching that moment?

One Thing at a Time

How many other things are you doing while you're working on a project? If you're anything like me, you're probably drinking a cup of coffee, eating a snack, listening to music, and picking up your phone to scroll aimlessly every five minutes. In our chaotic modern society, it's no surprise that we all feel as if we have to be doing ten things at once. It seems to be we ladies who get the most caught up in this constant cycle of trying to do it all. And who can blame us? For centuries, there's been an enduring narrative that women are better at multitasking than men.

Trying to Do It All

It's not hard to see why this multitasking woman stereotype exists. Just take a look at those mamas who coordinate the preschool routine with the efficiency of a drill sergeant, or the female CEO who's put out ten metaphorical fires before lunchtime, or the freelancer juggling multiple deadlines! This stereotype often works against us in the workplace, where research shows women are more frequently asked to complete tasks that don't help us get promoted than men are—and, of course, we are likelier to say yes.

But a study recently published in the journal *PLOS ONE* disproves the myth that women are better at multitasking than men. Turns out nobody is good at multitasking—not even us superwomen! What our brains are good at is switching between

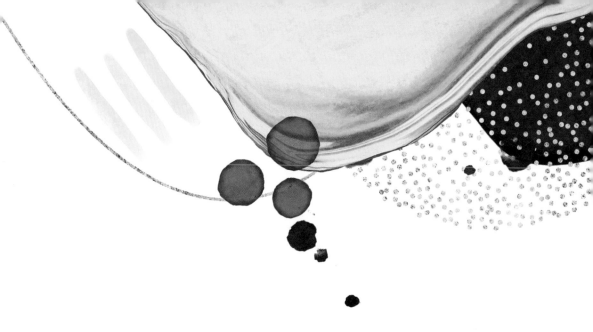

multiple tasks, which makes us feel like we're multitasking. In reality, our brains simply aren't designed to work on multiple tasks at a time—particularly if they're similar tasks that use the same part of the brain. So, while you might be able to get away with listening to a podcast while you're at the gym, you'd probably end up with a meaningless jumble of words if you tried to listen while writing an article (not speaking from experience or anything!). When you're trying to do everything, you're actually doing nothing.

When you're constantly switching between tasks, it drains your energy and disrupts your concentration. If you've ever felt super drained after a long, chaotic day and realized that you actually achieved a sweet lot of nada, that's probably because you were basically treading water by trying to do everything at once.

Catch Yourself Multitasking

As the name suggests, monotasking is the direct opposite of multitasking. If multitasking is the scatterbrained black sheep of the family who can't hold down a job, think of monotasking as the golden child who has their life together! Try to stay aware of when the multitasking monster creeps in so you can monotask instead. Next time you catch yourself doing it, ask yourself, "Is it really necessary that I do both of these things at once?" Try to prioritize which task is more important and complete it before you move on to the next one. Try this out in real life and record how it goes below.

What was I doing when I caught myself multitasking?

How was I feeling at the time?

Which task is more important?

When I prioritized and did one task at a time, how did it go?

What are some takeaways for next time I catch myself multitasking?

Productivity Sprints

Doing short, sharp bursts of work is the most effective way to put monotasking into practice. One popular technique is the Pomodoro Method, which involves using a timer (there are many browser extensions and apps you can use for this) to do timed 25-minute productivity sprints, separated by five-minute breaks. During those bursts, you focus solely on the task at hand—no emails, no social media, and no distractions. The delayed gratification of knowing that you can procrastinate to your heart's content during your break makes it so much easier to stay focused. Track your progress through a Pomodoro session below, and then reflect on how it worked out for you.

Sprint #1 (25-minute task, 5-minute break):

What task did I tackle?

What did I do for my break?

Sprint #2 (25-minute task, 5-minute break):

What task did I tackle?

What did I do for my break?

Sprint #3 (25-minute task, 5-minute break):

What task did I tackle?

What did I do for my break?

Sprint #4 (25-minute task, 5-minute break):

What task did I tackle?

What did I do for my break?

How well was I able to focus during the sprints? Did I finish my task?

What did I do during my breaks? Did this help me recharge?

Hold Yourself Accountable

When it comes to tackling our to-do lists and pursuing our goals, many of us have the best of intentions. But when the time comes to actually do it, we just don't feel like it! The reality is, sometimes the commitment you make to yourself just isn't enough. That's where external accountability comes in. This is when you tell a friend, family member, colleague, partner, or even a coach what goal or task you're going to be working toward. Then, they can check in with you to make sure you did it. Sometimes, just saying your goals out loud to someone else makes them feel real—so you believe in them yourself! Plus, knowing you're going to have to report back about your progress works wonders for keeping you on track. If it's a longer-term goal, you can set regular plans to check in—whether that's weekly, monthly, or quarterly.

What is my goal?

Who will help keep me accountable?

How often will they check in on my progress?

What would I like to have accomplished each time they check in?

When will I complete this goal?

How did this exercise go? Did having external accountability help me accomplish my goal?

Get In the Zone

Okay, so focusing solely on one task for even an hour can be easier said than done. I know this better than anyone—I'm the queen of distraction and often find myself drifting off into a daydream while in the middle of a conversation with someone. Whoops! The good news is, a few simple strategies go a long way in helping you get into the zone. For example, I absolutely swear by using my noise-canceling headphones while I'm in the middle of a deep work session. Use this exercise to brainstorm some strategies that might work for you!

What task am I trying to accomplish?

_____

_____

_____

_____

What strategies might help me focus during this task?

_____

_____

_____

_____

_____

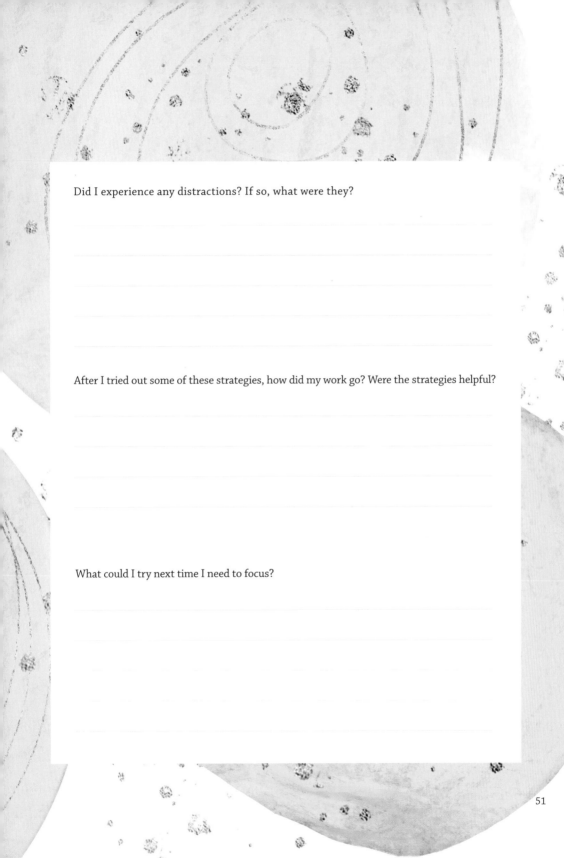

Did I experience any distractions? If so, what were they?

After I tried out some of these strategies, how did my work go? Were the strategies helpful?

What could I try next time I need to focus?

Conquer Your To-Do List

Want to become an absolute productivity ninja? This is where you combine all the mindful methods you've just read about—monotasking, productivity sprints, and accountability. Here's how to do it.

First, write down everything you need to do for the week ahead—even the little things like doing your laundry or sending off a package at the post office.

Identify whether there are any similar tasks you can batch together—whether it's replying to a bunch of emails or writing a couple of blog posts.

Determine on which days you're going to do which tasks—ideally keeping those similar tasks together.

Each morning, use an hour-by-hour planner or an app to split your tasks into hourly or half-hour chunks, factoring in some breaks. Try this out below:

Time	Task	Time	Task

Use a timer app to do your timed productivity sprints, eliminating all distractions during those sessions. Consider finding an accountability partner or using a program to keep you on track. At the end of the week, reflect on how well this productivity system worked for you.

Striving for Progress over Perfection

We've spoken a lot about being kind to yourself and cutting yourself some slack. After all, there's more to life than just ticking tasks off a to-do list. But it's important to know that this doesn't mean becoming complacent or "giving up" on yourself. Working to improve yourself doesn't mean there's anything wrong with your current state—it just means you have enough self-love to want to create the best possible life for yourself. You can love your body at any shape or size while still trying to become fitter and stronger. You can be okay with entering a new industry as an absolute beginner while trying to learn as much as you can. You can learn to enjoy your life on a tight budget while actively working on growing your wealth.

Acceptance and Improvement

Think about the types of people who are at the top of their respective fields, whether they're athletes, chefs, authors, or fashion designers. Do they win one gold medal, Michelin star, or Pulitzer Prize, then decide, "That's it, I can now go back to lying on my sofa and binge-watching Netflix for the next five years"? No! They're always tweaking and improving and working on their craft, even though they've already "made it" by most standards.

Author Danielle Steel is set to have published almost 200 books by her mid-seventies and still writes for 20 to 22 hours per day. Arnold Schwarzenegger still lifts weights in his seventies, despite having achieved international success as a bodybuilder in his twenties. These successful people know that striving for your goals isn't about reaching one destination where you can finally feel "perfect." It's about continually making progress (no matter where you're at) and the lessons you learn along the way.

The point is, whether you're 17, 27, or 70, it's absolutely possible to accept yourself exactly as you are, while simultaneously working to become the best version of yourself that you can be. That said, it's not always as easy as just flicking a switch! Here are some strategies to help you along the way.

Practice Self-Love

You can work on your self-worth by practicing kindness and compassion toward yourself—even when you feel like you've messed up or aren't "kicking goals" in life. Give yourself the permission to feel those feelings when things go wrong—whether that's sadness, frustration, or anger. It can also be helpful to have a self-love tool kit handy, filled with things that make you feel good and help you bounce back more quickly.

What recently went wrong for me, and how did I feel about it?

Here's a list of things that I can do for myself the next time something goes wrong to feel better about myself:

What recently went well for me, and how did I feel about it?

Here's a list of things that I can do for myself the next time something goes well, to celebrate my successes:

My Schedule

Many of us get so excited about our goals in the beginning that we try to do all of them at once. What's far more effective is implementing just one positive change at a time. So, you might decide to start by drinking more water. You can focus on doing that and only that, until after a few weeks or months, it becomes a habit and you don't have to think about it. Then, start layering on other positive habits, one by one. In this exercise, you'll pick just one positive habit you can implement today to get you one step closer to your goals, and track your progress over the next few weeks.

What is the habit I'm trying to implement?

Week 1 Tracker

Monday	Tuesday	Wednesday	Thursday	Friday	Saturday	Sunday

Week 2 Tracker

Monday	Tuesday	Wednesday	Thursday	Friday	Saturday	Sunday

Week 3 Tracker

Monday	Tuesday	Wednesday	Thursday	Friday	Saturday	Sunday

Week 4 Tracker

Monday	Tuesday	Wednesday	Thursday	Friday	Saturday	Sunday

How do I feel about my progress toward implementing this habit this month?

What other positive habits would I like to track in the future?

Track Small Wins

Just because you don't achieve your goals overnight doesn't mean you're not constantly growing and learning and getting better. At the end of the day, the person who makes small but steady advances toward their goals on a consistent basis is going to be far more likely to achieve them than the person who goes at it full throttle for a few months and then loses steam. Just like that height chart your parents had for you as a kid, make sure to take note of all those little wins—even if it's just picking up a few new words in a language you're learning, or going up a pound in your weights at the gym. You'll be able to look back at that progress and remember just how far you've come.

My Small Win   Date

My Small Win   Date

20 Actions Toward Your Goal

Whether consciously aware of it or not, massive action is the one thing that unites many of the world's most successful people. Coined by self-help guru Tony Robbins, this term refers to the concept of taking consistent action until you get your desired result. Many of us give up on our goals the second we hit a roadblock, deciding it's "just too hard" or "wasn't meant to be." But the idea behind massive action is that you keep trying different keys until you find the right one for the lock. In this exercise, you'll create a list of 20 different things you could do to work toward your goal, then work your way down the list. If none of those achieve the desired result, it's time to go back to the drawing board.

1. _____

2. _____

3. _____

4. _____

5. _____

6. _____

7. _____

8. _____

9. _____

10. _____

11. _____

12. _____

13. _____

14. _____

15. _____

16. _____

17. _____

18. _____

19. _____

20. _____

Check off Your Progress

You have (at least) 365 chances to get up and start working toward your goals. Treating each new day like a blank canvas is a great strategy to help you avoid "all-or-nothing" thinking. In this exercise, you'll see checkboxes for each day of the week for 12 full weeks. Check off the days you did something (no matter how big or small) to make progress toward your goals. It can be extremely motivating to see a streak of Xs in a row, but it's also a good reminder that you are still making progress even if you don't do it every day.

Dates: _____

Monday	Tuesday	Wednesday	Thursday	Friday	Saturday	Sunday

Dates: _____

Monday	Tuesday	Wednesday	Thursday	Friday	Saturday	Sunday

Dates: _____

Monday	Tuesday	Wednesday	Thursday	Friday	Saturday	Sunday

Dates: _____

Monday	Tuesday	Wednesday	Thursday	Friday	Saturday	Sunday

Dates: _____

Monday	Tuesday	Wednesday	Thursday	Friday	Saturday	Sunday

Dates: _____

Monday	Tuesday	Wednesday	Thursday	Friday	Saturday	Sunday

Dates: _____

Monday	Tuesday	Wednesday	Thursday	Friday	Saturday	Sunday

Dates: _____

Monday	Tuesday	Wednesday	Thursday	Friday	Saturday	Sunday

Dates: _____

Monday	Tuesday	Wednesday	Thursday	Friday	Saturday	Sunday

Dates: _____

Monday	Tuesday	Wednesday	Thursday	Friday	Saturday	Sunday

Dates: _____

Monday	Tuesday	Wednesday	Thursday	Friday	Saturday	Sunday

Dates: _____

Monday	Tuesday	Wednesday	Thursday	Friday	Saturday	Sunday

Create Your Self-Worth Mantra

Jot down a mantra of self-worth you can repeat to yourself in the mirror each morning. Having daily mantras can help remind you of your greatness as you go through the day. It'll also help you start your morning on the right note. The more frequently you repeat your mantra, the more you internalize the message and, ultimately, come to accept it as your inner truth. If you want to take this a step further, you can create a list of mantras and carry them with you on the go as small reminders. This is especially helpful for when you're having a rough day and need a quick pick-me-up.

Example: I love myself because of my imperfections, not in spite of them.

My mantra:

How do I feel when I repeat this to myself in the morning?

My list of mantras:

Embracing the Chaos

I would love to be the type of person with a spotlessly clean home, minimalist capsule wardrobe, perfectly styled hair, and zero unread emails. But in reality, my apartment currently resembles a junkyard with a growing floordrobe, I have four different inboxes screaming for attention, and my hair is one knot away from being a bird's nest. And you know what? That's totally fine! Because I know that I'm working toward my goals, taking care of my health, paying my bills, and being kind to the people around me—and that's all that matters. Despite what the curated world of Instagram might tell us, life isn't meant to be perfect, pristine, and meticulously ordered.

The Wabi-sabi Way

Although you wouldn't know it by their meticulous attention to detail or clockwork-like train timetables, the Japanese believe that embracing imperfection is a central part of life. So much so that they even have their own phrase to describe this philosophy: wabi-sabi.

Wabi-sabi is the art of embracing imperfection and impermanence. Wabi loosely translates to "understated elegance," while sabi translates to "taking pleasure in the imperfect." It's believed that the phrase originated with traditional tea ceremonies, as a way to describe well-loved yet charming teacups that had been chipped or cracked from use. While it was once mainly used to describe a rustic aesthetic style (especially in pottery), the meaning of the term has evolved and broadened over the years.

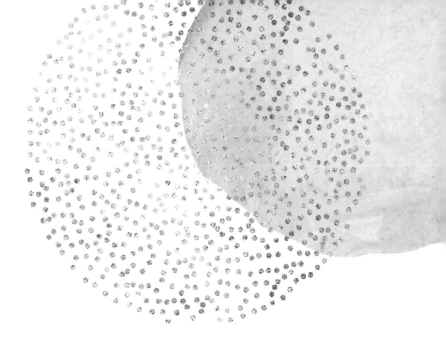

The concept of wabi-sabi is complex and nuanced, but there's a lot we can learn from it and apply to our everyday lives. First, there's the idea that you can find beauty in imperfection. Just like that teacup, you might have cracks and chips and bumps—we all do! But rather than trying to hide or fix them, wabi-sabi is all about embracing the beauty in those imperfections. The same goes for life. Rarely is it smooth sailing—in fact, it's a bumpier ride than a driver with their learner's permit! But you've got to go along for that ride and (gasp!) even learn to enjoy it, rather than resisting it.

Of course, coming to terms with this can be hard—especially when it feels like everyone else has it all together. So, here are a few simple strategies to help you embrace the chaos of life.

My Simple Pleasures

Make a list of 20 of those satisfying simple pleasures that bring you joy and comfort, whether it's the sound of the rain on the window when you're comfy in bed, the first magical sip of your coffee in the morning, or even the feeling of putting on warm clothes straight out of the dryer. Then, try to do them as often as possible and enjoy every second of it!

1.

2.

3.

4.

5.

6.

7.

8.

9.

10.

11.

12.

13.

14.

15.

16.

17.

18.

19.

20.

Quit the Comparison Trap

It's important not to beat yourself up for not having it all together. Because, despite what some social media accounts would have you believe, nobody does! So, next time you're giving yourself a metaphorical butt-kicking for not having abs like that Instagram model or a perfectly styled home like that mommy blogger, I suggest you give yourself a reality check instead. Remind yourself that you're only seeing the highlights reel of their lives (and what they want you to see), and you never really know what's going on behind closed doors. In this exercise, you'll note something you saw on social media that triggered the comparison trap for you, then reflect on what might be going on behind the scenes and how to counter your feelings of inadequacy.

What did I see on social media that triggered the comparison trap?

How did it make me feel?

What do I think might be going on behind the scenes of this post?

What is one good trait about myself that I love?

When I feel myself falling into the comparison trap, what can I do to counteract those feelings?

Reflect on the Unexpected

Trying to control every outcome in life can cause us a lot of unnecessary stress and inner turmoil. Often, we do this from a place of fear—we're afraid of the unknown, so we try to do everything in our power to steer things in the ideal direction. And yes, there are some things in life you can control, but there are many, many other things you can't. Sometimes you just have to surrender to the randomness of life rather than exhausting yourself trying to paddle in the opposite direction. Spend some time reflecting on some of the amazing yet unexpected things that have happened to you throughout your life. Maybe you didn't get a job you thought you really wanted, but the dream job you didn't know existed popped up soon afterward. Or maybe you were disappointed when you missed out on a trip, but met the love of your life back home. These "sliding doors" moments—unexpected events that alter the trajectory of our lives—are a great reminder that sometimes, the universe has our back.

An event in my life that I didn't expect:

Something good that happened because of this event:

An event in my life that I didn't expect:

Something good that happened because of this event:

An event in my life that I didn't expect:

Something good that happened because of this event:

Cultivate Resilience

Resilience is an ability to bounce back from anything life throws at you. How do you cultivate this, exactly? Well, much like any muscle in your body, it gets stronger the more you use it. People who have been through a lot of adversity in their lives naturally tend to be more resilient than those who haven't. But thankfully, even if you've led a pretty blessed life, it's never too late to build this important life skill. In this exercise, you'll think through five key ways to build resilience when you encounter a setback in your life.

A recent setback in my life:

_____

_____

_____

Optimism: What's the (realistic) best-case scenario in this situation?

_____

_____

_____

_____

_____

Perspective: How can I put this situation into perspective? What do I still have to be grateful for?

_____

_____

_____

_____

_____

_____

_____

Self-confidence: What is another challenge I've faced in the past, and how did I overcome it?

Connection: Who do I have in my support network who can help me get through this?

Decisive action: What concrete actions can I take to improve my situation?

Get Out of the Loop

When something "bad" happens, do you find yourself playing it repeatedly in your mind as if it's on loop? This is known as rumination, and it's often what prevents us from moving on from adversity. The practice of expressive writing can help you stop spinning your wheels and gain valuable insights from the challenges of life, which is essential for building resilience. Set a timer for 20 minutes, and in the space below, word-vomit all the thoughts and feelings you have about the situation. Give yourself permission to write badly and without inhibition—it's not meant to be a masterpiece, but rather an exploration of your innermost feelings. Feel free to grab another sheet of paper if you need more space!

Designing Your Perfect Day

We all have 24 hours in a day. That's 1,440 minutes, or 86,400 seconds. When you put it that way, it sounds like a lot, right?! Why is it, then, that some people seem to be able to fit a week's worth of goal-kicking into a day, while others spend half an hour just trying to find a matching pair of socks in the morning? (Oh, and don't get me wrong—you can absolutely be both people. I know I am!)

Conquer Your Schedule

Let me begin by acknowledging the fact that productivity is, of course, a privilege. There is a plethora of factors that can affect how much someone can realistically get done in a day— like their family situation, health problems (both mental and physical), financial issues, and so forth. For a single mom who's just trying to make it from paycheck to paycheck to support three kids, or someone who is caring for a family member, their main goal might just be to make it through the day.

That said, with the right resources, each and every one of us has the power to become an absolute productivity machine. Not

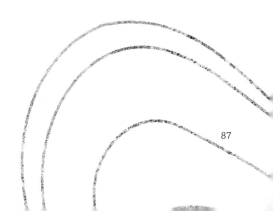

the type of person who works day and night to get everything done, because that's no fun! But rather, the woman who whizzes through her entire to-do list by 5 p.m. and still has the time and energy to hit the gym/go for mojitos/binge-watch five episodes of her favorite show—whatever tickles her fancy.

Show your schedule who's boss by making it work for you—not the other way around!

Hack Your Body Clock

We all have a biological clock ticking away in our brains that dictates our peak times for creativity and focus. By working with—not against—this predisposition, you can hack your biological clock and create your ideal schedule. Whether you're a morning person, a night person, have an all-around great sleeping schedule, or struggle to fall asleep, finding what works best for you will help you create an ideal schedule. Spend a week keeping a diary of the times of day when you feel most alert and energized, as well as the times where you find yourself nearly dozing off at your desk, along with what task or activity you were in the middle of at the time. Also take note of what foods and drinks you consumed around those times, as this can affect your energy levels. By being mindful of what's going on in your body, you can start to get a feel for your own biological clock.

Time	Task/Activity	Energy Level	Food/Drink Consumed

Time	Task/Activity	Energy Level	Food/Drink Consumed

Time	Task/Activity	Energy Level	Food/Drink Consumed

Time	Task/Activity	Energy Level	Food/Drink Consumed

Time	Task/Activity	Energy Level	Food/Drink Consumed

Time	Task/Activity	Energy Level	Food/Drink Consumed

Time	Task/Activity	Energy Level	Food/Drink Consumed

Create a Magnificent Morning Routine

Whether you're a rise-with-the-sun or sleep-til-nine kinda gal, having a morning routine in place can be extremely beneficial. It helps kick-start your energy and focus, and sets you up for a more productive day. There's no right or wrong way to start your day, but by picking an activity or two from the categories below, you can create your own well-rounded morning routine that sets you up for success.

Movement: Getting active in the morning has been shown to boost your energy levels and keep them firing all day long. Write a few ideas below for ways to add movement to your morning routine. *Examples: YouTube workout, going for a walk, hitting the gym, doing yoga, solo dance party.*

Mindfulness: This is anything that involves focusing solely on the present moment. Write a few ideas below for ways to add mindfulness to your morning routine. *Examples: meditation, gratitude journaling, getting outdoors, your skin care routine, simply enjoying your coffee.*

Mind: If you're going to absorb any external information in the morning, you may as well make it count! Write a few ideas below for ways to engage your mind during your morning routine. *Examples: listening to an educational or entertaining podcast or an audiobook, reading a great book or magazine.*

Elevate Your Evening Routine

How you finish your day is just as important as how you start it! Whether you're an early bird or a night owl, having a solid morning routine in place will help you wind down for the night and improve your quality of sleep. Below, you'll see a list with some ideas of what you can add to your evening routine. Once you've looked it over, write out your own plan for an evening routine that will work for you.

- Have a cup of decaf tea.
- De-stress in the bathtub.
- Listen to relaxing music.
- Read a book or listen to a calming audiobook.
- Listen to a "bedtime story": these are boring stories specifically created to help you drift off to sleep.
- Write down three things you were grateful for or learned that day.
- Do a brain dump of all the thoughts or worries running through your mind.
- Set yourself up for a successful morning by writing out your goals and tasks for the next day.

My evening routine:

After you tried out this evening routine for a few days, what effects did you notice?

Supercharge Your Sleep

While it's awesome to find your ideal bedtime and have a solid evening routine in place, it's not going to do much if your sleeping conditions aren't up to scratch. What you do once you get into bed is just as important—if not more so—than what you do before it. Optimizing your sleeping conditions and habits is vital for ensuring that you get a good night's rest and wake up feeling refreshed. Below, you'll see a list with some ideas: look it over, then write out your own sleep strategy.

- Ensure your bedroom and linen are the right temperature. We tend to sleep better when we're on the cooler side; try keeping layers on the bed so you can adjust.
- Don't watch the clock. It's a good idea to remove or hide all visible clocks in the bedroom.
- Don't force yourself to try to sleep if you're genuinely not tired. If it's been more than 20 minutes and you're not feeling it, get out of bed and go read or listen to something boring (no screens!).
- Block out light with blackout blinds or a sleep mask. If you have too much light filtering into your bedroom, it prevents your brain from getting the message that it's sleep time.
- If you have a lot of noise pollution in your area, try using earbuds or a white noise machine.
- Avoid caffeine after 2 p.m., including coffee and black tea.
- It's important that your body comes to associate bed with sleep. So, try to use it for only two things—sleeping and being intimate. That means no reading, no scrolling on your phone, and definitely no using your laptop!

My sleep strategy:

After you tried out this sleep strategy for a few days, what effects did you notice?

Make Your Schedule Work for You

You're one of a kind—which means your daily routine should be just as unique as you are. By creating a schedule that fits your needs, biological clock, and lifestyle, you can start operating at your full potential without feeling overworked or overwhelmed! To start designing your schedule, ask yourself the questions below. Then, you can use your calendar app or download a spreadsheet and fill out the time slots for your day.

What time will I wake up?

What part of my morning routine will be nonnegotiable (e.g. movement or mindfulness practice)?

When will I do my hardest task for the day?

When will I do my most creative work?

What time will I have my daily meals?

How will I spend my lunch break? What will help me recharge for the afternoon?

When and how will I exercise?

How will I wind down for the evening? When will I switch off my devices?

What time will I go to bed?

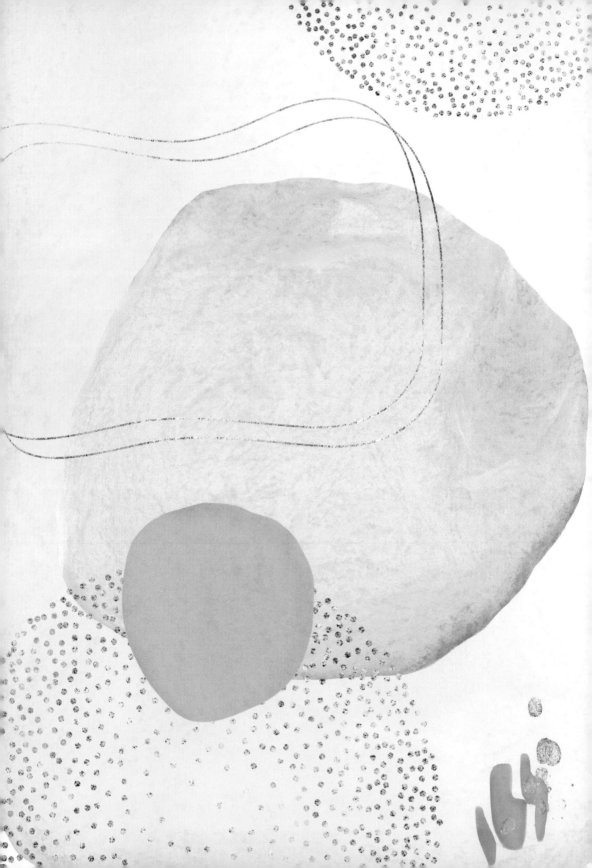

Mindfulness Beyond Meditation

Do you ever feel as if you're just going through life on autopilot? Zipping from task to task, appointment to appointment, without ever really stopping to smell the roses (or, you know, even just take a breath!)? When life gets busier than Sephora during a Black Friday sale, you might find that's when you start to "drop the ball." It's leaving your smartphone on the subway, spacing out on where you parked your car, missing deadlines, or forgetting to make your daughter a cake for the bake sale. Hey, it happens to even the most organized type-A people among us!

Meditation and Mindfulness: What's the Difference?

The answer to dealing with our busy lives isn't necessarily to do less, because sometimes, that's just not an option. The answer is to practice mindfulness—and no, that doesn't have to mean meditation!

Mindfulness and meditation are kind of like Doritos and dip. That is, you need mindfulness to practice meditation (properly, anyway), but you don't necessarily need meditation to practice mindfulness. Sure, meditation is one of the oldest and most well-known ways to practice mindfulness, but it's not the only way.

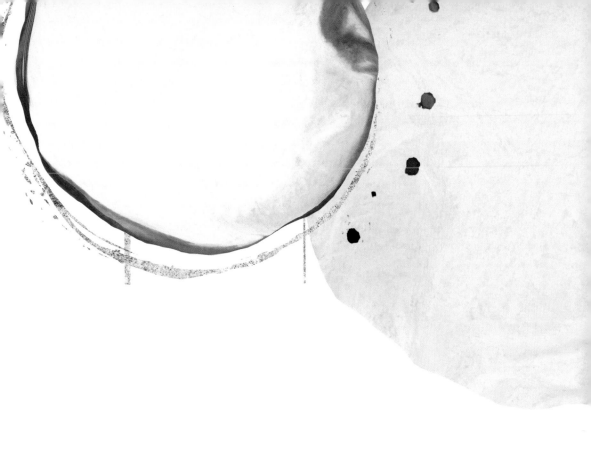

That's not to say that I have anything against meditation—I personally use an app for my 15-minute morning meditations and absolutely love it. Sure, it took a little while to find a guided meditation app with a voice that didn't make me want to hurl my phone against the wall. I also prefer to lie down with a blanket over myself for my meditation, because I'm pretty much incapable of sitting upright before I've had my morning coffee (sleeping meditation is a thing, right?!). But now I'm sold!

Tame Your Monkey Mind

Mindfulness helps us tame the monkey mind—not by suppressing your unconscious thoughts, but by giving them the space to be heard. By acknowledging—not judging—these thoughts during moments of quiet reflection, you can begin to question why it is you're having them. In this exercise, choose any mindfulness technique to practice, then answer the following prompts.

During my mindfulness practice, what limiting beliefs entered my mind?

Were these facts, or just thoughts?

Are there any events or indisputable facts in my life that could prove them untrue?

How can I recognize these thoughts and gently release them next time they surface?

Try a Walking Meditation

Lace up your sneakers and head outside—whether it's to a nearby park, beach, or just around your neighborhood. The location isn't that important. The key here is to focus on the sensations of your body: the sound of your breath entering and leaving your body, the movement of your hands swinging by your side, the feeling of your feet coming into contact with the ground.

What did I see?

What did I hear?

What did I smell?

_____

_____

_____

_____

What did I feel?

_____

_____

_____

_____

How did I feel at the end of this meditation?

_____

_____

_____

_____

Mindfulness in the Everyday

Practicing mindfulness doesn't have to be time-consuming or difficult. Often, it's something you can incorporate into things you're already doing (the only type of multitasking you can get away with!). In this exercise, you'll try bringing mindfulness to two everyday activities: your skin-care routine, and washing the dishes.

As you go through your skin-care routine, focus on the sensations you feel on your skin and the scent of the product. What do you notice? How does it feel to reflect on these sensations?

As you wash the dishes, focus on the scent of the soap, the feeling of the suds, the temperature of the water, and the shape and design of the dishes. What do you notice? How does it feel to reflect on these sensations?

If you can, try to practice one or both of these mindfulness exercises over the course of a week. How do you feel after making this time for everyday mindfulness?

Write it Out

If you're more of a word person than a visual one, journaling is another excellent way to tap into your present moment awareness. This could mean jotting down things you're grateful for or how you're feeling or even just doing "flow of consciousness" journaling where you put down anything (no matter how strange it might seem!) that comes to mind. The important thing is that you don't police yourself—you're not writing for anyone but yourself. Use the space below to write whatever you want—just let the words flow until you fill the space, and see how you feel at the end.

Find Your Mindful

So, how do you know when you're on to a winner? After all, mindfulness isn't just something you practice once and then never do again. The idea is for it to become a natural part of your life, much like showering or brushing your teeth (which can also be mindfulness activities!). Here are some questions to ask yourself to help determine whether you've found the right fit.

What mindfulness practice did I try?

Do I enjoy it?

How does it make me feel afterward?

Can this easily fit into my lifestyle?

A Mindful Life

Once you've found your go-to way to practice mindfulness, you can start to integrate it into other aspects of your life. After all, the benefits go beyond just your focus and mood—you can use mindfulness to up level your health, productivity, relationships, and more. In the sections below, reflect on the mindfulness practices you've learned in this workbook so far, and brainstorm ways you can incorporate mindfulness into many different areas of your life.

How can I bring mindfulness into my work day?

How can I bring mindfulness into my relationships?

How can I bring mindfulness into my sleep routine?

How can I bring mindfulness into my relationship with my body and my fitness routine?

How can I bring mindfulness into my relationship with food and eating?

Setting Boundaries

Okay, so it's one thing to have all these amazing goals, productive routines, and mindful practices in place. But what happens when other people get involved, steal your time, and kill your vibe? It could be your sister who demands that you pick her up from the airport when you had already planned to spend the day working on a project. Or the client who insists on calling you at one-hour intervals throughout the day, rather than just writing a simple email. Or the partner who guilts you for not spending enough time with them, even though you just spent the last five nights together. If there's one thing that's certain in life, it's that you can't control what other people do and think. However, what you can control is how you react to them—and a major part of that is setting personal boundaries.

What Are Personal Boundaries?

When you think of boundaries, you might think of a physical separation like a brick wall or barricade. But while personal-space boundaries are important, this isn't about putting a wall up around yourself. It's about teaching the people around you what you are and aren't willing to accept. Everyone has their limits, and it's important to figure out what yours are—and to stick to them. You wouldn't just willingly let someone you know steal money from your bank account, right? Well, why would you let them do it with your time and energy?

They're equally limited resources and, some would argue, even more valuable—after all, you can always make more money, but you can never get your time back.

Protect your time and energy like you do your money. They're just as important! It's important to set boundaries in all aspects of your life; otherwise, you'll feel as if you're being pulled in a thousand different directions, like a half-price designer purse at a sample sale.

What Depletes Your Energy?

You need to protect yourself from things that deplete your time and energy, including these:

- Pointless distractions
- Last-minute requests that aren't really urgent
- Things you don't enjoy doing but feel obligated to do
- People who ask too much of you when you already have a lot on your plate

In this exercise, you'll identify some of these energy-depleting situations, and brainstorm ways to avoid them.

What was a situation recently where I felt my time and energy were being wasted?

Is this kind of situation something that comes up often for me? What are some other examples of this happening?

Event:

Total time spent:

How much of this time was really necessary?

Next time, how might I set a boundary to avoid wasting time this way?

Event:

Total time spent:

How much of this time was really necessary?

Next time, how might I set a boundary to avoid wasting time this way?

Event:

Total time spent:

How much of this time was really necessary?

Next time, how might I set a boundary to avoid wasting time this way?

Boundaries in Your Romantic Relationships

Boundaries and intimacy might seem as if they'd be sworn enemies, but they go hand in hand. In order to foster strong communication and respect in your relationship, it's important to establish clear boundaries from the get-go. This can include big relationship things like cheating or yelling or being nasty during an argument, or smaller, day-to-day stuff like not having to clean the entire house by yourself. But personal boundaries can also just be about your personal needs, whether that's 15 minutes of quiet time to yourself every day or being able to do something that's important to you each week. This one is particularly important if you're a parent! By having this conversation up front, your partner doesn't have to play guessing games about what you want and need. Below, take some space to plan out your boundaries and how to have this conversation with your partner.

What boundaries do I need to set with my partner?

When will we have this conversation?

Where will we have this conversation?

How did the conversation go?

Boundaries for Friendships and Family

It's just as important to set boundaries in other relationships in your life. Family can be tough, because the power dynamics are often deeply ingrained, and it can take a little extra work to change them. When it comes to friends, this issue often presents itself in the form of accepting favors or attending things out of obligation. When this happens, it's important to take those family members or friends aside and gently tell them that although you love them, the current situation is negatively affecting you. Then you can inform them of your new boundaries. Establish the new boundaries and stick to them, so they know you're not messing around!

What boundaries do I need to set with my family member or friend?

When will we have this conversation?

Where will we have this conversation?

How did the conversation go?

129

Learning to Say No

There's a bit of an art to saying no to people graciously and respectfully. Yelling "No!" into the phone or slamming doors in people's faces probably isn't going to win you any friends. But you also don't need to apologize profusely for not bending over backward to make someone happy. Nor do you need to make excuses or instill false hope by saying "maybe next time!" if you have zero intention of doing so. It can be a simple as saying to them, "Thank you so much for thinking of me for this, but unfortunately, I won't be able to make it as I have other commitments/too much on my plate at the moment." Use this space to brainstorm some ways to say no, then see how it goes when you use these techniques in real life.

Ways I could say no:

How did it go when I tried this out?

Is there anything I could do differently next time?

Setting Tech Boundaries

I'm calling it: email and social media notifications are the two biggest time and energy leeches of them all! While back in the day people had to log in to a desktop computer to check their emails or feeds, smartphones and 4G Internet mean we're now all constantly available at any time of the day. This means that the line between our work and personal lives is blurrier than a selfie after a few cocktails. Let's face it—smartphones aren't going anywhere soon, and if anything, they're just going to become a more inextricable part of our personal identities. That's why it's up to you to set your own personal boundaries around the way you use technology. In this exercise, you'll test out a few techniques for setting tech boundaries.

Try setting a time after you get up and/or before you go to bed when you're not allowed to touch your phone. After you've done this for one week, reflect here on how it went:

Turn off all of your notifications. Yes, all of them—even your emails! If you have to carve out a few small exceptions for work or safety, go ahead, but otherwise nothing is so important that it can't wait. After you've done this for one week, reflect here on how it went:

Consider blocking your apps. There are some great apps out there that allow you to block your access to distracting apps within certain time periods or after a certain amount of use. After you've done this for one week, reflect here on how it went:

Finding Your Boundaries

If you're not used to setting boundaries, it can be hard to know what yours are. Sometimes, we get so used to doing things to please others that we lose touch with what we really want—and what we don't. By doing this mindfulness exercise, you can tap into what is and isn't serving you so you can set appropriate boundaries. Next time someone asks you for a favor, find a quiet spot and ask yourself these questions.

The task:

How will I feel if I take on this task?

Am I doing this out of guilt?

Is this my duty or responsibility?

Am I comfortable doing this?

What would I have to sacrifice?

You Can Do Anything, Not Everything

There's never been a better time in history to be a woman. While it can be argued that we still have a long way to go, we have more freedom, equality, and opportunity than ever before. Whether it's being the CEO of a company, leader of the free world (hey, we'll get there one day!), or the head of your own household, women can be whatever or whoever they want to be—and that's an amazing feeling! However, in a time when women can do anything, it's easy to feel like we should be doing everything.

The Downside of Doing It All

Starting a family, running a business, training for a marathon, and learning a language all at once? Why the heck not?! Running a blog and a podcast, writing a book, working four days a week, freelancing, and trying to stay fit? Sure thing! (Okay, so maybe that last one is me.)

In a time when women #runtheworld, it's easy to feel like in order to be productive, you have to be doing all things at once. But as much as you'd look amazing in spandex and a cape, you're not Superwoman. None of us are! And just like multitasking, trying to work toward too many goals at once can backfire more spectacularly than a cheesy pickup line.

If everything is a top priority, then nothing is a priority. After all, they're called "priorities" because they're supposed to be more important than everything else! When you're balancing

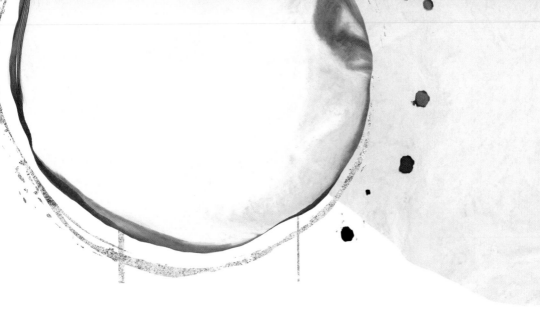

many different things at once, something is eventually going to tip the scales. Meaning: it's pretty much impossible to give all of them an equal amount of love, time, and attention. Usually, one of two things happens as a result. The first is that one of the things slips down the list and gets neglected for months (for many of us, that's our gym routines), and the second is that we spread ourselves too thin and end up doing a subpar job at all of them. Either way, it doesn't leave us feeling good or putting our best work into the world. The other downsides of trying to do too many different things at once include constant feelings of overwhelm, increased stress and anxiety, and making some of those silly mistakes I mentioned earlier. On an extreme level, it can also lead to burnout, which we'll delve into in the next chapter.

But don't worry, I've got you covered! In this chapter, I'll share my top tips for slowing down a little—and feeling okay about it.

Stay in Your Lane

The reason we often get so caught up in the hamster wheel of life (that is, running and running and getting nowhere) is the dreaded comparison trap. And, as always, social media is the biggest enabler. It's far too easy to look at your social media feeds and think everyone is doing so much more than you are. It's enough to make even the most confident gal feel lazy or stuck. Consider doing a digital declutter of any of the social media accounts, pages, or groups that constantly make you feel that you need to be doing more. Here, it's important to note the difference between people who inspire and motivate you, and those who simply make you feel anxious and overwhelmed every time they pop up in your feed. If it's the latter, hit unfollow—and if it's someone you know in real life and you're worried about offending them, just unfollow (not unfriend) or hide them from your feed.

Accounts that make me feel anxious and overwhelmed:

After I unfollowed or blocked these accounts, how did I feel when looking at social media?

What else in my life makes me fall into the comparison trap?

Are there ways I could avoid these things?

The 80 Percent Rule

I'm a serial project starter. I come up with all these crazy ideas (in the shower, in my dreams, on the bus, wherever!) and want to immediately put them all in action. Do you know how many of these projects I ended up actually finishing? Precisely zero. There's absolutely nothing wrong with coming up with loads of ideas—it's part of being a creative person. The issue is when you have so many different things on the go that you can't dedicate a significant amount of time to any one of them. That's why I've implemented the 80 percent rule. Basically, this means you have to have nearly finished your project before you can move on to another one. Below, try this out with a task or project, and record how it goes.

What task or project am I trying to complete?

At what point will I have finished 80 percent of the project?

After I focused on getting 80 percent of the project finished, how easy was it to complete the rest?

Do I think this technique will be helpful in finishing other projects or tasks in the future?

Pick Your Three Things

We've all felt that sense of impending doom when looking at a daily to-do list longer than our forearm. When we have too many different things to get done, we often don't know where to start, and soon we are finding ways to procrastinate. The solution? Pick three things you want to get done today. At the end of the day, make a habit of writing down what you achieved and the biggest lessons you learned. Reflecting on this helps facilitate self-growth and reminds you of how much progress you're making—even if it feels insignificant at the time.

What are my three things to get done today?

What did I end up achieving today?

What lessons did I learn?

The Urgent/Important Matrix

If you struggle to figure out which tasks you should prioritize, Eisenhower's Urgent/Important matrix will be your new best friend. This concept was inspired by Dwight Eisenhower, the 34th president of the United States. This is a simple yet effective way to figure out which tasks you should focus on and which ones you should delegate or ignore.

Urgent and Important	Urgent But Not Important
Top priorities, do before everything else.	*Short timeline, but can be delegated.*

Important But Not Urgent

Prioritize these once the urgent/important tasks are done.

Not Important and Not Urgent

Time wasters—drop these tasks from your list!

Go From Doing to Being

We find ways to busy ourselves even when we don't actually have anything to do! The solution? Focus on being, not doing. This is when instead of trying to fix or improve or achieve anything, you're simply existing in the present moment. That's not to say that you have to stare at a blank wall for hours on end—that would be boring as heck! But it's about just giving yourself permission to enjoy when you're being without really doing anything, whether that's watching TV or hanging out with a friend. In this exercise, you'll brainstorm some mantras to help you stay in the present moment, then see how it feels to just be.

What mantra could I use to stay in the present moment?

Examples: "I am exactly where I need to be right now" or "I give myself permission to enjoy this moment."

When I tried this out in a real-life situation, how did it go?

How do I feel when I'm able to focus on being, not doing?

_____

_____

_____

_____

_____

_____

_____

What can I change about my everyday life to make it easier to stay present?

_____

_____

_____

_____

_____

_____

_____

Learning to Rest, Not Quit

A chieving your goals isn't always easy. If it were, everyone would do it! There will always be days when you really don't feel like getting out of bed for that early morning run or working on that side hustle when you've had a long day at the office. And hey, most of the time when you just get started, you'll find that it wasn't nearly as bad as you thought it would be! But there are other times when you really are that exhausted and mentally drained to the point where you'd be doing yourself a disservice to push through. And that's totally okay!

Recharging Your Batteries

As touched on earlier, you're human and you have limitations. In times like these, it can be easy to feel like throwing in the towel—to tell yourself you're just not cut out for this, or that you don't want to do it anymore. Here's when it's important to learn to rest, not quit.

When you've truly got nothing left in your tank, there's absolutely nothing wrong with taking a day or even a week off from your goals. Think about professional athletes—they have rest and recovery built in as non-negotiable parts of their training schedules. This gives their muscles the chance to repair and grow between workouts and gives them a chance to recover, both physically and psychologically. You can do the same when it comes to your goals by taking a step back when you need to.

Say you're a freelancer and you're almost feeling ready to go back to the stability of an office job because the constant hustle is getting you down. By putting a pause on chasing new clients for, say, a week, you might find that you come back with a renewed sense of energy and purpose. It's kind of like when you take a vacation and you weirdly find yourself looking forward to getting back into the office! You've given yourself the chance to recharge your batteries, and now you're firing on all cylinders again.

Recognize Burnout

Burnout is a state of extreme mental, physical, and emotional exhaustion, caused by excessive and chronic stress. Stress is the body's natural reaction to any change that requires an adjustment or a response, and it can sometimes be a good thing when it comes to getting stuff done. However, when left unmanaged long term, stress can lead to burnout, which is when you feel so emotionally drained that you find it difficult to complete your work or even get out of bed in the morning. Some signs of burnout include:

- Feeling extremely negative, cynical, or demoralized about work
- Experiencing reduced workplace performance or efficiency
- Experiencing an ongoing lack of motivation and energy
- Feeling tense, irritable, and on edge
- Experiencing forgetfulness and reduced ability to focus

What burnout symptoms have I noticed in my own life?

What situations tend to make these burnout symptoms appear or worsen?

When will I know when it's time to take a break?

How long will I take a break for?

How will I get back on track when the break is over?

Listen to Your Body

Our bodies are pretty amazing. When you're doing too much and on the brink of exhaustion, your body has a multitude of different ways of telling you it's time to slow down. Some of the early physical warning signs of burnout include:

- Frequent headaches or jaw pain from clenching
- A twitching eye
- Digestive issues
- Body aches
- Constantly feeling tired
- Changes in appetite
- Insomnia
- Weight gain or weight loss
- Increased illness like colds and the flu

What signs have I noticed in my own body when I start feeling burned out?

What has been helpful in the past for improving these symptoms?

Next time I notice myself feeling this way, what can I do to take care of myself?

Practice Self-Care

At the crux of it, self-care is taking the time to tend to your own emotional, psychological, and physical needs. So, what does that entail, exactly? Well, there's not one definition because self-care can mean completely different things to different people. It's anything that energizes you, relieves your stress, and makes you feel more like yourself again. In this exercise, you'll brainstorm self-care strategies to help you bounce back from burnout. Under the four headings below, list some activities you can do to nourish your mind, body, soul, and spirit. Then, commit to picking one or two to try every day.

Mind

Body

Soul

Spirit

Brimming with creative inspiration, how-to projects, and useful information to enrich your everyday life, Quarto Knows is a favorite destination for those pursuing their interests and passions. Visit our site and dig deeper with our books into your area of interest: Quarto Creates, Quarto Cooks, Quarto Homes, Quarto Lives, Quarto Drives, Quarto Explores, Quarto Gifts, or Quarto Kids.

First published in 2021 by Rock Point, an imprint of The Quarto Group,
142 West 36th Street, 4th Floor, New York, NY 10018, USA
T (212) 779-4972 F (212) 779-6058 www.QuartoKnows.com

Rock Point titles are also available at discount for retail, wholesale, promotional, and bulk purchase. For details, contact the Special Sales Manager by email at specialsales@quarto.com or by mail at The Quarto Group, Attn: Special Sales Manager, 100 Cummings Center Suite 265D, Beverly, MA 01915 USA.

10 9 8 7 6 5 4 3 2 1

ISBN: 978-1-63106-819-5

Publisher: Rage Kindelsperger
Creative Director: Laura Drew
Managing Editor: Cara Donaldson
Senior Editor: Katharine Moore

Printed in China

This book provides general information on various widely known and widely accepted self-care and wellness practices. However, it should not be relied upon as recommending or promoting any specific diagnosis or method of treatment for a particular condition, and it is not intended as a substitute for medical advice or for direct diagnosis and treatment of a medical condition by a qualified physician. Readers who have questions about a particular condition, possible treatments for that condition, or possible reactions from the condition or its treatment should consult a physician or other qualified healthcare professional.

LEFT

BEHIND

The Judgments

Neil Wilson and Len Woods

MOODY PUBLISHERS

CHICAGO

Produced with the assistance of the Livingstone Corporation (www.LivingstoneCorp.com). Project staff includes Len Woods, Neil Wilson, Ashley Taylor, Kirk Luttrell, Mary Horner Collins, Mark Wainwright, Carol Barnstable, and Rosalie Krusemark.

ISBN:0-8024-6455-6

1 3 5 7 9 10 8 6 4 2

Printed in the United States of America

Contents

For the latest information on other Left Behind series and Bible prophecy products, go to www.leftbehind.com. Sign up for a free e-mail update!

Foreword

Tim LaHaye and Jerry B. Jenkins

Jesus said, "Watch and wait" (Mark 13:32–37).

Even believers looking for the coming of Christ will be surprised at the Rapture. But it will be a delightful surprise—the fulfillment of our deepest longings. One of our goals in the Left Behind novels is to keep others from being surprised in the worst sense—by being caught off guard and left behind.

A large body of literature written in the last half century highlights the growing evidence that Christ's coming is quickly drawing near. We have written several books ourselves seeking to help people understand biblical passages about the end times. *Are We Living in the End Times?* (Tyndale), *The Tim LaHaye Prophecy Study Bible* (AMG), *Will I Be Left Behind?* (Tyndale), and *Perhaps Today* (Tyndale) all were written to help people understand biblical prophecy.

The Left Behind Bible study guide series from Moody Publishers uses material from the novels to illustrate an introduction to Bible prophecy. Authors Neil Wilson and Len Woods emphasize that the Left Behind stories are rooted in biblical themes. They bring together various prophetic passages of Scripture and plenty of thought-provoking questions, with the goal of getting you to live in the light of the imminent return of Christ.

These studies will help you discover what we wanted to show in the novels—that all the historical, technological, and theological pieces of the puzzle recorded in biblical prophecy are more plainly in place for Christ's return now than ever before. Technological advances commonplace today parallel scriptural pictures in such an uncanny way that they allow for prophesied events that even a generation ago seemed impossible.

Biblical prophecy doesn't look nearly as strange anymore. Our intent in the novels was to simply make the truth of the Bible come alive for fiction readers. That many people have been driven back to their Bibles is a wonderful outcome. In your hands is another vehicle that allows you to closely study the Bible texts that thrilled us and served as the basis for the fiction. We encourage you to become a wise student of God's Word and a watchful observer of the times.

Introduction

Neil Wilson and Len Woods

Welcome to this introductory study of end-times prophecy! We pray that you will find these studies helpful, challenging, and encouraging in your walk with Christ.

General interest in prophecy among Christians tends to behave very much like an active volcano. About once in each generation, seismic events in history grab everyone's attention, and the internal pressure to see events from God's point of view causes an eruption of prophetic concerns. Early in our generation toward the end of the 1960s, we experienced just such an eruption with the turbulence surrounding the Vietnam conflict, the heating up of the Cold War, the rise of the Jesus Movement, and the publication of Hal Lindsay's book *The Late Great Planet Earth,* among other things. Larry Norman's song "I Wish We'd All Been Ready" struck a chord of longing and urged our generation to get serious about Jesus. He was coming like a thief in the night. Prophetic students pointed to the rebirth of the nation of Israel and the rapidly closing time period following that event as an indisputable clue to Christ's coming. We tried to get ready—for a while.

Unfortunately, like many examples of public fascination, the wide interest in prophetic issues gradually dwindled to the faithful remnant, who continually read the signs of the times and served the body of Christ with urgent warnings. The volcano seemed to go silent. Here and there, prophecy conferences still gathered. Books were written, papers presented, and even heated arguments raged behind closed doors. The world quickly went on its way to more hopeful outlooks: the fall of the Berlin Wall, the explosive rise of the stock market, and murmured promises that the world might finally be headed toward life as a kinder, gentler place. Continual background trouble was ignored. Even the body of Christ seemed fascinated with herself. The potential of church growth achieved by appealing to seekers and making it very easy to slide into the church created an atmosphere where judgment and Christ's second coming sounded a little harsh and unfriendly. The church became, in many ways, too successful to long for rapture. The distant rumble of the volcano was drowned out by the music of worship that too often sounded a lot more like entertainment than serious consideration of the majesty of God.

The arrival of new centuries and the much rarer dawn of new millenniums have usually created a suspicion that more than just a calendar time line might be coming to an end. Recently, terms like Y2K became shorthand for fearful brooding over the sudden realization that our entire civilization seemed dependent on countless computers remaining sane in spite of a simple change in their internal clocks. Many expected a cyber meltdown. Some predicted a new Dark Ages. Thousands stockpiled food, water, and guns. And most of us wondered what would happen. Christians who knew prophecy simply couldn't see cataclysmic Y2K scenarios indicated in the Bible. Their more or less confident counsel to trust in God's sovereignty was often met with suspicion and derision by those practical believers, whose motto seemed to be "God helps those who help themselves." Y2K caught the church unprepared.

In the predawn jitters of the new millennium, a book was published that seemed to almost instantly grab the imagination of millions. *Left Behind* became plausible fiction. As Tim LaHaye and Jerry Jenkins have repeatedly stated, one of their primary goals was to demonstrate that all the technology was already in place to allow prophetic events to occur that previous generations had found inconceivable. A volcano of interest in prophecy began to rumble. The tremors found their way to the shelves of the largest general market bookstores as millions of the *Left Behind* books left the stores. Many Christians reported surprise over their own lack of understanding of what seems so apparent throughout Scripture. In the years that have followed the publication of the first novel, there has been a healthy movement toward greater acknowledgment that God has a plan for this world, and a deadline is approaching. His Word makes that fact clear, and the events of history are providing confirming echoes.

We trust these studies will tune your heart and mind to the purposes of God. We hope that as a result of studying his Word you will long for your daily life to harmonize with God's purposes. We pray that you increasingly will be intent on doing what God has set before you, glancing from time to time at the horizon, anticipating your personal encounter with the Lord! May your prayers frequently include, "Maranatha!"—Lord, come quickly!

How to Get the Most from Your Study

Depending on your background and experiences, the Left Behind studies will

- Help you begin to answer some important questions that may have occurred to you as you were reading the Left Behind novels,

- Introduce you to the serious study of biblical prophecy,

- Provide you with a starting point for a personal review of biblical prophecy that you remember hearing about as you were growing up, or

- Offer you a format to use in meeting with others to discuss not only the Left Behind novels but also the Bible texts that inspired the stories.

If you are using these studies on your own, you will establish your own pace. A thoughtful consideration of the Bible passages, questions, and quotes from the Left Behind series and other books will require a minimum of an hour for each lesson.

If you will be discussing these lessons as part of a group, make sure you review each lesson on your own. Your efforts in preparation will result in a number of personal benefits:

- You will have thought through some of the most important questions and be less prone to "shallow answers."

- You will have a good sense of the direction of the discussion.

- You will have an opportunity to do some added research if you discover an area or question that you know will be beyond the scope of the group discussion.

- Since a group will probably not be able to cover every question in each lesson because of time constraints, your preparation will allow you to fill in the gaps.

Tools to Use

- Make sure you have a Bible you can read easily.

- Most of the quotes in these studies come from the New Living Translation. If your Bible is a different version, get in the habit of comparing the verses.

- Consider reading some of the excellent books available today for the study of prophecy. You will find helpful suggestions in the endnotes.

- Put some mileage on your pen or pencil. Take time to write out answers to the questions as you prepare each lesson.

- Continually place your life before God. Ultimately, your study of prophecy ought to deepen your awareness of both his sovereignty and compassion. You will appreciate the overwhelming aspects of God's love, mercy, and grace toward you even more as you get a wider view of his grandeur and glory.

Leading a Group Through the Left Behind Studies

Leading a Bible study on prophecy can be daunting to any teacher. When it comes to prophecy, all of us are students; we've all got a lot to learn. Approaching this study as a fresh opportunity to ask questions, to seek the Lord and his Word for answers, and to help others in the process will take the burden of being "the teacher" off your shoulders.

Remember that it's helpful to be confident in what you know as long as you're not confident you know everything. The study of prophecy does bring up many questions for which the most honest answer is, "We don't know." God has, however, given us more information in his Word than he is often given credit for. To use the apostle Paul's language, we may see some things sharply and other things dimly, but that's so much better than being in the dark. Take a careful look at Tim LaHaye's article "How to Study Prophecy," and encourage your group to read it. It provides valuable guidelines as you prepare for these discussions.

No matter the level of knowledge you or your group may have, set your sights on increasing your group's interest in the study of prophecy as well as deepening their commitment to living for Christ. Keep your group focused on the need to know Jesus better. Ultimately, it's hard to get excited about expecting a stranger. The more intimately we get to know Jesus, the more we long to see him. Consider using as a motto for your group the words of Paul, "Yet I am not ashamed, because I know whom I have believed, and am convinced that he is able to guard what I have entrusted to him for that day" (2 Timothy 1:12 NIV).

Prophecy and evangelism travel together. A study like this can provide unexpected opportunities to share the gospel. We tend to think that evangelistic conversations are primarily a backward look with a present application—God has accomplished certain gracious things through Christ and his death and resurrection; therefore, what shall we do today? Prophecy reverses the discussion, creating a forward look with a present application—God promises he will do these things tomorrow; therefore, how shall we live today? Be prayerfully alert to opportunities during and after studies to interact seriously with group members about the state of their souls. Tim LaHaye and Jerry Jenkins have letters from hundreds of readers of the Left Behind series who came to faith in Christ in part as a result of their exposure to prophecy. Pray that God will use your study to accomplish his purposes in others' lives, including yours.

Several Helpful Tools

Bibles: Encourage group members to bring and use their Bibles. We've quoted in the workbook the verses being discussed in each lesson, but having the full context of the verses available to examine is often helpful. We recommend that you have on hand for consultation at least one copy of a trustworthy study Bible that highlights prophetic issues, such as the *Ryrie Study Bible* (Moody Press) or the *Tim LaHaye Prophecy Study Bible* (AMG Publishers).

Bible Concordance and Bible Dictionary: Each of these tools can assist a group in the process of finding specific passages in Scripture or gaining a perspective on a particular biblical theme or word.

Resource Books: The endnotes for each lesson include a number of books from which insightful quotes have been drawn. If members in your group have access to these books, encourage them to make the volumes available for others to read.

Left Behind Novels: Because there are several editions of the books, you may discover some discrepancies in the page listings of the quotes from the novels and the particular books you have. A little search of the pages nearby will usually get you to the right place.

Hints for Group Sessions

1. Encourage participants to review and prepare as much of each lesson as they are able in advance. Remind them it will help the learning process if they have been thinking about the issues and subjects before the session.
2. As you prepare the lessons, decide what questions you will make your focus for discussion. Unless your time is open-ended and your group highly motivated, you will not be able to cover every question adequately in an hour.
3. Only experience with your particular group will give you a sense of how much ground you can cover each session.
4. Consider appointing different group members to ask the questions. That will take the spotlight off you and allow them to participate in a comfortable way.
5. Take time in each session for feedback and questions from the group. These spontaneous reflections will give you a good sense of how much the group is learning, integrating, and being affected by the lessons.

The Place of Prayer

Make it a point to pray with the group and for the group during the study. Use part of your preparation time to bring each person from the group before God in prayer. Open and close each session by asking God, who alone knows the full meaning of every prophecy he has inspired in his Word, to open your hearts and minds to understand and respond in practical, wholehearted ways to the truth of Scripture.

How to Study Bible Prophecy

Tim LaHaye

Prophecy is God's road map to show us where history is going. The Bible's predictions claim literal and specific fulfillments that verify that such prophecies are indeed from God. The key to interpreting Bible prophecy is in discerning what is literal and what is symbolic. Therefore, the best way to avoid confusion in the study of prophetic Scripture is to follow these simple directions:

1. Interpret prophecy literally wherever possible. God meant what he said and said what he meant when he inspired "holy men of God [who] spake as they were moved by the Holy Ghost" (2 Peter 1:21 KJV) to write the Bible. Consequently we can take the Bible literally most of the time. Where God intends for us to interpret symbolically, he makes it obvious. One of the reasons the book of Revelation is difficult for some people to understand is that they try to spiritualize the symbols used in the book. However, since many Old Testament prophecies have already been literally fulfilled, such as God turning water to blood (Exodus 4:9; 7:17–21), it should not be difficult to imagine that future prophetic events can and will be literally fulfilled at the appropriate time. Only when symbols or figures of speech make absolutely no literal sense should anything but a literal interpretation be sought.

2. Prophecies concerning Israel and the church should not be transposed. The promises of God to Israel to be fulfilled "in the latter days," particularly those concerning Israel's punishment during the Tribulation, have absolutely nothing to do with the church. The Bible gives specific promises for the church that she will be raptured into heaven before the Tribulation (John 14:2–3; 1 Corinthians 15:51–52; 1 Thessalonians 4:13–18).

3. For symbolic passages, compare Scripture with Scripture. The Bible is not contradictory. Even though written by numerous divinely inspired men over a period of sixteen hundred years, it is supernaturally consistent in its use of terms. For example, the word "beast" is used thirty-four times in Revelation and many other times in Scripture. Daniel explains that the word is symbolic of either a king or kingdom (see Daniel 7–8). By examining the contexts in Revelation and Daniel, you will find that "beast" has the same meaning in both books. Many other symbols used in Revelation are also taken directly from the Old Testament. These include "the tree of life" (Revelation 2:7; 22:2, 14), "the Book of Life" (Revelation 3:5), and Babylon (Revelation 14:8ff.).

Some symbols in Revelation are drawn from other New Testament passages. These include terms such as "the word of God" (1:2, 9ff.), "Son of Man" (1:13; 14:14), "marriage supper" (19:9), "the bride" (21:9; 22:17), "first resurrection" (20:5–6), and "second death" (2:11;

20:6, 14; 21:8). Other symbols in Revelation are explained and identified in their context. For example, "Alpha and Omega" represents Jesus Christ (1:8; 21:6; 22:13); the "seven candlesticks" (1:13, 20) are the seven churches; the "dragon" is Satan (12:3ff.); and the "man child" is Jesus (12:5, 13).

Though some prophetic passages should be interpreted symbolically, it is important to remember that symbols in the Bible depict real people, things, and events. For example, the "seven candlesticks" in Revelation 1 represent real churches that actually existed when the prophecy was given.

Keeping the three points above in mind will provide you with a confident approach to prophetic Scriptures and guard against a multitude of errors. Allow God's Word always to be your final guide.

(Adapted from the *Tim LaHaye Prophecy Study Bible*, AMG Publishers, used with permission.)

Overview of the End Times

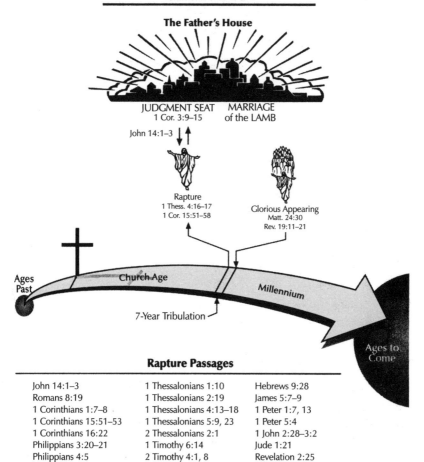

End-Times Overview
Matthew 24:29–31

The Father's House

JUDGMENT SEAT
1 Cor. 3:9–15

MARRIAGE
of the LAMB

John 14:1–3

Rapture
1 Thess. 4:16–17
1 Cor. 15:51–58

Glorious Appearing
Matt. 24:30
Rev. 19:11–21

Ages
Past

Church Age

Millennium

7-Year Tribulation

Ages to
Come

Rapture Passages

John 14:1–3	1 Thessalonians 1:10	Hebrews 9:28
Romans 8:19	1 Thessalonians 2:19	James 5:7–9
1 Corinthians 1:7–8	1 Thessalonians 4:13–18	1 Peter 1:7, 13
1 Corinthians 15:51–53	1 Thessalonians 5:9, 23	1 Peter 5:4
1 Corinthians 16:22	2 Thessalonians 2:1	1 John 2:28–3:2
Philippians 3:20–21	1 Timothy 6:14	Jude 1:21
Philippians 4:5	2 Timothy 4:1, 8	Revelation 2:25
Colossians 3:4	Titus 2:13	Revelation 3:10

Second Coming Passages

Daniel 2:44–45	Mark 13:14–27	1 Peter 4:12–13
Daniel 7:9–14	Mark 14:62	2 Peter 3:1–14
Daniel 12:1–3	Luke 21:25–28	Jude 1:14–15
Zechariah 12:10	Acts 1:9–11	Revelation 1:7
Zechariah 14:1–15	Acts 3:19–21	Revelation 19:11–20:6
Matthew 13:41	1 Thessalonians 3:13	Revelation 22:7, 12, 20
Matthew 24:15–31	2 Thessalonians 1:6–10	
Matthew 26:64	2 Thessalonians 2:8	

LEFT
BEHIND

The Judgments

Lesson 1
Here Comes the Judge!

1. You are conducting random interviews at a shopping mall, asking the question: "How would you describe God?" Which of the following answers do you think people would most commonly give?

   a   Creator   f)   Lord
   b) Spirit   g)   Father
   c) Judge   h)   Friend
   d) Savior   i)   Other
   e) King

2. Of the following adjectives, which description of God is dominant in *your* mind?

   a) loving   h)   compassionate
   b) powerful   i)   all-knowing
   c) merciful   j)   patient
   d) forgiving   k)   stern
   e) vengeful   l)   distant
   f) sovereign (i.e., in control)   m) other
   g) angry

3. Now read through the lists above again, this time noting the answers you would expect if you asked churchgoers those questions after a Sunday service. How might their ideas about the nature of God differ from the population in the mall?

   _____

   _____

   _____

4. Why do you think courtroom reality TV shows are perennially popular in our culture? In what ways do they represent a deep human yearning for true accountability and justice?

_____

_____

_____

_____

_____

_____

_____

Unfolding the Story

(*Left Behind,* pp. 310–12)

The first book in the Left Behind series features a small group of people (including a minister) who are trying to discover what will happen now that millions have suddenly disappeared from the earth. The minister, Bruce Barnes, leads the confused bunch in a serious study of the Bible so they can be prepared for what is yet to come. Here's a scene from one of their first few get-togethers:

> "LET ME JUST BRIEFLY OUTLINE the Seven-Sealed Scroll from Revelation five, and then I'll let you go. On the one hand, I don't want to give you a spirit of fear, but we all know we're still here because we neglected salvation before the Rapture. I know we're grateful for the second chance, but we cannot expect to escape the trials that are coming."
>
> Bruce explained that the first four seals in the scroll were described as men on four horses: a white horse, a red horse, a black horse, and a pale horse. "The white horseman apparently is the Antichrist, who ushers in one to three months of diplomacy while getting organized and promising peace.
>
> "The red horse signifies war. The Antichrist will be opposed by three rulers from the south, and millions will be killed."
>
> "In World War III?"
>
> "That's my assumption."
>
> "That would mean within the next six months."
>
> "I'm afraid so. And immediately following that, which will take only three to six

months because of the nuclear weaponry available, the Bible predicts inflation and famine—the black horse. As the rich get richer, the poor starve to death. More millions will die that way."

"So if we survive the war, we need to stockpile food?"

Bruce nodded. "I would."

"We should work together."

"Good idea, because it gets worse. That killer famine could be as short as two or three months before the arrival of the fourth Seal Judgment, the fourth horseman on the pale horse—the symbol of death. Besides the postwar famine, a plague will sweep the entire world. Before the fifth Seal Judgment, a quarter of the world's population will be dead."

"What's the fifth Seal Judgment?"

"Well," Bruce said, "you're going to recognize this one because we've talked about it before. Remember my telling you about the 144,000 Jewish witnesses who try to evangelize the world for Christ? Many of their converts, perhaps millions, will be martyred by the world leader and the harlot, which is the name for the one world religion that denies Christ.

"The sixth Seal Judgment," Bruce continued, "is God pouring out his wrath against the killing of his saints. This will come in the form of a worldwide earthquake so devastating that no instrument would be able to measure it. It will be so bad that people will cry out for rocks to fall on them and put them out of their misery." Several in the room began to weep. "The seventh seal introduces the seven Trumpet Judgments, which will take place in the second quarter of this seven-year period."

5. According to Bruce (and Revelation 5–6), what events lie just ahead for both the post-Rapture world and their group (which dubs itself the "Tribulation Force")?

_____

_____

_____

_____

_____

_____

_____

_____

6. Which of the following terms best describe Bruce's tone: grim, hopeful, or matter-of-fact? Why?

_____

_____

_____

_____

_____

_____

Back to Reality

Most of us face trials and uncertainty—everything from broken-down cars and job layoffs to chronic illnesses and the loss of loved ones. But what would it be like to be left behind at the Rapture, and then to realize that what you thought was odd and farfetched turned out to be true? To know that because the first incredible event has occurred, that the entire world is about to endure a series of devastating judgments unparalleled in human history?

It is hard to imagine being in *that* situation. Perhaps helping people to visualize and even feel the desperation and despair of such a situation explains one of the strongest attractions for people reading the Left Behind novels.

7. How do you think you might feel if you found yourself left behind? What might you do? Did the novels accurately convey what you would expect to experience?

_____

_____

_____

_____

_____

_____

8. When you read about these horrible events, how, if at all, does it affect your view of God?

_____

_____

9. How do you reconcile God's divine and righteous judgment with God's divine love and mercy?

_____

_____

_____

_____

_____

A God of Wrath?

A God of wrath—the words seem contradictory. What does it mean that God, who describes himself as love (1 John 4:8), is also a being filled with wrath? How do we reconcile these ideas? Perhaps the following thoughts will be helpful:

> The flip side of God's righteousness is his wrath against evil. Certain aspects of human character elicit God's wrath. It is the response of his holiness to all wickedness and rebellion. . . . God cannot tolerate sin because his nature is morally perfect. He cannot ignore or condone such willful rebellion. He wants to remove the sin and restore the sinner, but the sinner must not distort or reject the truth. . . . God shows his anger from heaven against those who persist in sinning.[1]

Charles Ryrie reminds us that sometimes two ideas or concepts don't fit easily together because they operate in sequence: "wrath results when grace is rejected."[2]

Understanding the Word

One of the great principles of correct Bible interpretation is to take the whole counsel of God (i.e., the entire Bible) into consideration before coming to any conclusions. In other words, it is possible—if we focus only on one or two passages—to develop an incomplete and inaccurate picture of how things really are. Far too many people do this. They read, for example, a few verses about God's judgment, and they form a wrong, warped view of the character of God.

Howard Hendricks, the legendary Bible teacher from Dallas Seminary, said the best way to avoid distorting the message of the Bible is to compare Scripture with Scripture: "That offers the greatest safety net, because the greatest interpreter of Scripture is Scripture itself. . . . [T]he more you compare Scripture with Scripture, the more the meaning of the Bible becomes apparent. The parts take on meaning in light of the whole."[3]

Following the advice of Dr. Hendricks, let's compare the grim revelation of coming wrath and judgment (Revelation 6–18) with this passage from 2 Peter 3:3–15:

> *First, I want to remind you that in the last days there will be scoffers who will laugh at the truth and do every evil thing they desire. This will be their argument: "Jesus promised to come back, did he? Then where is he? Why, as far back as anyone can remember, every-thing has remained exactly the same since the world was first created." They deliberately forget that God made the heavens by the word of his command, and he brought the earth up from the water and surrounded it with water. Then he used the water to destroy the world with a mighty flood. And God has also commanded that the heavens and the earth will be consumed by fire on the day of judgment, when ungodly people will perish.*
>
> *But you must not forget, dear friends, that a day is like a thousand years to the Lord, and a thousand years is like a day. The Lord isn't really being slow about his promise to return, as some people think. No, he is being patient for your sake. He does not want any-one to perish, so he is giving more time for everyone to repent. But the day of the Lord will come as unexpectedly as a thief. Then the heavens will pass away with a terrible noise, and everything in them will disappear in fire, and the earth and everything on it will be exposed to judgment.*
>
> *Since everything around us is going to melt away, what holy, godly lives you should be living! You should look forward to that day and hurry it along—the day when God will set the heavens on fire and the elements will melt away in the flames. But we are looking for-ward to the new heavens and new earth he has promised, a world where everyone is right with God.*
>
> *And so, dear friends, while you are waiting for these things to happen, make every effort to live a pure and blameless life. And be at peace with God.*
>
> *And remember, the Lord is waiting so that people have time to be saved.*

10. What do these paragraphs from Scripture tell you about what is to come following the Rapture of the church?

_____

_____

_____

_____

_____

11. What do these paragraphs tell you about the nature of God?

_____

_____

_____

_____

12. Does God intend to severely judge the ungodly? Why? Given how corrupt the world is, why hasn't God already poured out his judgment?

_____

_____

_____

_____

_____

_____

Next, ponder this verse:

Notice how God is both kind and severe. He is severe to those who disobeyed, but kind to you as you continue to trust in his kindness. But if you stop trusting, you also will be cut off. (Romans 11:22)

Consider also this Old Testament passage prophesying the coming of Messiah. Note carefully all that is foretold of his ministry:

The Spirit of the Lord GOD is upon me, because the LORD has anointed me to bring good news to the afflicted; He has sent me to bind up the brokenhearted, to proclaim liberty to captives and freedom to prisoners; to proclaim the favorable year of the LORD and the day of vengeance of our God. (Isaiah 61:1–2 NASB; see also Luke 4:18–19)

13. What do the two passages above add to your understanding of the true nature of God? Are they contradictory, or complementary (showing the various facets of God's character)?

_____

_____

_____

_____

_____

_____

Finding the Connection

If we fail to remember God's long-suffering patience; if we forget his countless attempts down through the centuries to woo his rebellious creatures to himself; if all we do is focus on the terrible events of the Tribulation period, we will develop a twisted understanding of God's heart. With so much violence and death prophesied for the end of the world, many fall into this devilish trap. They wrongly conclude that he is an angry, vindictive deity. Consequently they either avoid him or attack him—calling into question his person and his plans.

The characters in the Left Behind series try to keep God's love and mercy in view. They are deeply thankful for their salvation, and they make it their aim to tell others the good news of forgiveness in Christ.

14. Christians do not have to worry about God's wrath. Christ took the severest of punishments upon himself and gave believers his eternal life and favor. With this in mind, how should followers of Jesus be motivated by the truth of the "wrath of God"? What difference does that make in _your_ life?

_____

_____

_____

_____

_____

John 3:36 says:

And all who believe in God's Son have eternal life. Those who don't obey the Son will never experience eternal life, but the wrath of God remains upon them.

15. How does this verse alter the way you look at your non-Christian neighbors, friends, and/or family members?

_____

_____

_____

_____

_____

_____

_____

"While this period is primarily a time of wrath and judgment, it also features a very strong note of mercy and grace—a note that too often gets overlooked. Sometimes . . . God gets a 'bad rap' when people focus exclusively on the judgments and terrors to come. They see the Lord as some kind of angry monster, heaping up catastrophes and pouring them on the heads of defenseless, innocent men and women, like an obnoxious child might pour gasoline down a teeming anthill with one hand while getting ready to drop a lit match with the other.

"But this is all wrong! First, those who suffer the judgments of God in the Tribulation are not 'innocent men and women.' . . . [T]he rebels alive at that time will not only reject God and his offer of salvation but will run greedily toward every vile sin known to man, including blasphemy of a kind beyond description. And second, despite their gross sin, God intends that these Tribulation judgments *might lead even these wicked sinners to faith in his Son, Jesus Christ!*"[4]

Tim LaHaye and Jerry B. Jenkins

Making the Change
(Tribulation Force, pp. 63–64)

Tough, terrible times lie ahead for the world. Things will get much, much worse before they ever get better. Forget the chorus of optimistic voices who insist that mankind will somehow figure out a way to live in peace and harmony. That will not take place until Christ returns in ruling glory. Anyone who asserts otherwise is deluded at best, a false prophet at worst.

Here's how pastor Bruce Barnes summed up the beginning of that climactic period of divine judgment:

> "**WE'VE ALREADY MISSED THE RAPTURE,** and now we live in what will soon become the most perilous period of history. Evangelists used to warn parishioners that they could be struck by a car or die in a fire and thus they should not put off coming to Christ. I'm telling you that should you be struck by a car or caught in a fire, it may be the most merciful way you can die. Be ready this time. Be ready. I will tell you how to get ready.
>
> "My sermon title today is 'The Four Horsemen of the Apocalypse,' and I want to concentrate on the first, the rider of the white horse. If you've always thought the Four Horsemen of the Apocalypse was a Notre Dame football backfield, God has a lesson for you today. . . .
>
> "During these seven years, God will pour out three consecutive sets of judgments—seven seals in a scroll, which we call the Seal Judgments; seven trumpets; and seven bowls. These judgments, I believe, are handed down for the purposes of shaking us loose from whatever shred of security we might have left. If the Rapture didn't get your attention, the judgments will. And if the judgments don't, you're going to die apart from God. Horrible as these judgments will be, I urge you to see them as final warnings from a loving God who is not willing that any should perish."

"There will be a great 'soul harvest' during the Tribulation. Uncounted millions of men and women and girls and boys will recognize that, although they missed the Rapture and thus will have to endure the terrors of the Tribulation, yet God is still calling them, wooing them to His side. And through the ministry of the Holy Spirit, these individuals will respond in repentance and faith and will choose to forsake their rebellion and instead commit their lives and their futures into the hands of the Lord Jesus Christ. . . . And do not forget: Every one of these new believers will have been left behind after the Rapture precisely because he or she had (to that point) rejected God's offer of salvation. Yet even then, the Lord will not give up on them. Even then, He will use whatever means necessary—fire, blood, earthquakes, plague, war, famine, persecution—to jolt them out of their spiritual slumber and into the waking enjoyment of His glorious light.

"Far from being a stomach-turning display of divine meanness, the Tribulation demonstrates beyond all doubt that our holy God is also a God who loves beyond all human reckoning."[5]

Tim LaHaye and Jerry B. Jenkins

16. What is the message from the novel for those who still have not opened their hearts and lives to Jesus Christ?

_____

_____

_____

_____

_____

_____

_____

17. How should believers live in light of the certainty of immediacy of these events?

_____

_____

_____

_____

_____

_____

_____

18. Do you know beyond a shadow of a doubt that Jesus is your Savior? Are you following him as Lord of your life? If you answered no to either question, what are you waiting for? Why the delay?

_____

_____

_____

_____

_____

_____

_____

Becoming a Christian

You are not a Christian because you live in a so-called "Christian nation." You are not a Christian because you are involved (either superficially or deeply) in a Christian church. You are a Christian when Jesus Christ is in your life— when he is your life. How does this happen? How does Christ come to live in us? Does he sneak in? Barge in? No, he comes when we acknowledge our need for him and open our lives to him. He comes when we trust him to be our Savior.

A Christian understands he can't DO anything to deserve Christ's lavish offer of forgiveness and eternal life. On the contrary, she understands that Jesus has already DONE everything necessary to bring rebellious, messed-up people like ourselves into a right relationship with the one true God. Salvation is a gift (Ephesians 2:8–9). This gracious, surprising overture on the part of God is a no-strings-attached offer. We either take it by faith, or we reject it. To say "maybe later, but not right now" is the same as saying "no."

If you've been putting off this most important of all decisions, perhaps you'd like to pray right now along these lines:

> Lord Jesus, I need you. I admit that until this moment I have lived for myself and I have ignored you and shut you out of my life. I need you. I need forgiveness and peace. I need the life that only you can give. I believe that you died in my place and paid for my rebellious and foolish acts. I believe that you rose from the dead and stand ready to move into my life. I accept you as my Savior and King and Friend. Thank you for loving me and making me a child of God. Begin to change me now into the person you want me to be.

If you pray that prayer (or one like it) and are sincere, you can be sure that Jesus will forgive you, give you eternal life, and take up residence in your life. This is how we become true children of God.

Pursuing the Truth

Ezekiel 18:31 says:

> *Put all your rebellion behind you, and get for yourselves a new heart and a new spirit. For why should you die, O people of Israel?*

19. What does this statement from God to his people Israel show you about the heart of God?

_____

_____

_____

_____
_____
_____
_____
_____

20. What aspect of God's character as "Judge" do you still not understand or continue to wrestle with?

_____
_____
_____
_____
_____

"I run into people who are really blown away that I and the other faculty of a theological seminary can't explain everything in the Bible. So I usually provoke their thinking with a question: Does it really bother you that I as a finite person cannot fully understand an infinite Person? Does that really bother you? It would bother me more if I could, because then I wouldn't need God. I'd be as smart as He is.

"Don't get tied up in knots over the problems and unanswerable questions that come up in your study of the Bible. The miracle is that you can understand all the essential things that God wants you to understand for your eternal salvation and for your daily living."[6]

Howard Hendricks

21. What is the chief lesson you are taking away from this study?

_____
_____
_____
_____
_____
_____

22. List the names of the people in your life with whom you can share what you've learned in this lesson. Pray for these folks. Ask God to give you an opportunity to speak with them about spiritual matters.

_____

_____

_____

_____

_____

_____

_____

Lesson in Review . . .

- A terrible time of judgment awaits those living during the Tribulation.
- These judgments reveal the holiness of God and his wrath against the stubborn rejection of his grace.
- These judgments reveal the great patience of God and his fervent desire for sinners to turn to him and find life.
- In light of what is to come, Christians need to warn this generation of the consequences of unbelief and the blessings of trusting in Christ.

LEFT
BEHIND

The Judgments

Lesson 2
The Day of the Lord

1. What was one of the *best* days of your life, thus far? Why?

_____

_____

_____

_____

_____

_____

2. What was one of the *worst* days of your life? What happened?

_____

_____

_____

_____

_____

_____

Unfolding the Story
(*Tribulation Force*, pp. 373–74)

The Left Behind novels use fictional characters and biblical facts to portray life on earth following the Rapture—that "could-happen-at-any-moment" event in which all true believers in

Jesus will be "caught up" to meet the Lord in the air. The "heroes" of the twelve-book series are a small band of individuals who have put their faith in Christ after the Rapture. These new believers have no choice but to watch and wait as the prophesied end-times events begin to unfold like clockwork.

In this scene from the second book in the series, reporter Buck Williams witnesses the Antichrist signing a peace treaty with Israel. This momentous event signals the beginning of the end.

[O]THER LEADERS MADE INNOCUOUS SPEECHES and rattled on about the importance and historicity of the document they were about to sign. Several decorative pens were produced as television, film, video, and still cameras zeroed in on the signers. The pens were passed back and forth, the poses struck, and the signatures applied. With handshakes, embraces, and kisses on both cheeks all around, the treaty was inaugurated.

And the signers of this treaty—all except one—were ignorant of its consequences, unaware they had been party to an unholy alliance.

A covenant had been struck. God's chosen people, who planned to rebuild the temple and reinstitute the system of sacrifices until the coming of their Messiah, had signed a deal with the devil.

Only two men on the dais knew this pact signaled the beginning of the end of time. One was maniacally hopeful; the other trembled at what was to come.

At the famed Wall, the two witnesses wailed the truth. At the tops of their voices, the sound carrying to the far reaches of the Temple Mount and beyond, they called out the news: "Thus begins the last terrible week of the Lord!"

The seven-year "week" had begun.

The Tribulation.

3. How did the world's hunger for peace and Carpathia's promise of peace pave the way for the moment described above?

_____

_____

_____

_____

_____

_____

4. In the Left Behind books, what events follow this promising, hopeful event?

_____

_____

_____

_____

_____

Back to Reality

Charles Ryrie defines the Day of the Lord as "an extended period of time, beginning with the tribulation and including the events of the second coming of Christ and the millennial kingdom on earth."[1] Dr. Mark Bailey, president of Dallas Theological Seminary, expands on this:

> The Day of the Lord is a period of time when God's judgment and salvation are revealed, a time when He directly intervenes in history. If one looks at the concept of a "day" from a Jewish perspective, it is composed of two parts: an evening and a morning. . . . There is darkness on the one half; there is light on the other. And the same is true for the period of time referred to as the Day of the Lord.
>
> The darkness represents the judgment that will come during a seven-year period known as the Tribulation. The light represents a period of blessing that will be the kingdom age or, as it is called because of its length, the Millennium—the thousand-year reign of Christ on earth. Several passages of Scripture talk about the Day of the Lord as a period of judgment or blessing.[2]

5. What world events do you see unfolding today that might be signs the Rapture is near?

_____

_____

_____

_____

_____

6. Do you feel fearful about the future, or confident that God is in control? Explain.

_____

_____

_____

_____

_____

7. What does the world's obsession with religious tolerance and its outrage at any suggestion of moral absolutes likely mean for Christians who try to discuss the coming judgments of God?

_____

_____

_____

_____

_____

Wake-Up Call!

"For years some men have been talking as if they *thought* the end were near, but at the beginning of the Tribulation they will *realize* that the end is actually at hand. Scientists, politicians, and even church leaders warn today that the end of human history could be upon us, and even use the term 'Armageddon,' but people are not behaving as if they believe it. Real estate is being bought and sold, savings are being accumulated, and plans are continually being made for the future. But when the Tribulation comes, people will hide in bomb shelters and will actually seek death rather than try to preserve life. The future, in those days, will hold no attraction." [3]

Charles Ryrie

Understanding the Word

The Bible is replete with references to the coming "Day of the Lord." This future event is mentioned in thirteen of the sixteen prophetic books of the Old Testament, in more than one hundred separate passages. This repetition surely tells us that God wants us to understand this monumental period of time. Note the following classic passage:

[The LORD says], "That terrible day of the LORD is near. Swiftly it comes—a day when strong men will cry bitterly. It is a day when the LORD's anger will be poured out. It is a day of terrible distress and anguish, a day of ruin and desolation, a day of darkness and gloom, of clouds, blackness, trumpet calls, and battle cries. Down go the walled cities and strongest battlements!

"Because you have sinned against the LORD, I will make you as helpless as a blind man searching for a path. Your blood will be poured out into the dust, and your bodies will lie there rotting on the ground."

Your silver and gold will be of no use to you on that day of the LORD's anger. For the whole land will be devoured by the fire of his jealousy. He will make a terrifying end of all the people on earth. (Zephaniah 1:14–18)

8. Go back through the above passage and highlight the descriptive phrases used to describe this time. What themes do you see? What images are used?

_____

_____

_____

_____

_____

9. How is this a *terrifying* picture? In what ways is this a *comforting* reminder to you?

_____

_____

_____

_____

_____

10. Look at the worldwide chaos that ensued on September 11, 2001, when four jetliners crashed, hitting three buildings in two American cities. Compare the reaction to that event with the worldwide destruction and chaos prophesied above.

_____

_____

_____

_____

_____

_____

_____

_____

The Day of the Lord Described

The so-called "Day of the Lord" mentioned repeatedly in the Bible is given a number of sobering designations. Among them are:

- "day of disaster" (Deuteronomy 32:35)
- "a strange, unusual thing" (Isaiah 28:21)
- "a time of terror" (Jeremiah 30:7)
- "the time of Jacob's distress" (Jeremiah 30:7 NASB)
- "a time of anguish greater than any since nations first came into existence" (Daniel 12:1)
- "the great time of testing" (Revelation 3:10)
- "the time of your wrath" (Revelation 11:18)
- "God's wrath" (Revelation 15:1)
- "the terrible wrath of God" (Revelation 15:7)

Finding the Connection

By studying the Bible, poring over books on theology, and consuming old sermon tapes and videos, the new Christians in the Left Behind series are able to piece together what the immediate future held. They quickly realized that, according to God's eternal plan, worldwide judgment was imminent! Things on earth would be getting much worse (the Tribulation) before getting better (the Second Coming and the millennial rule of Christ)!

11. Why do human beings innately hunger for justice? Why do we feel disturbed when an obvious criminal escapes punishment on a technicality?

_____

_____

_____

_____

12. Think of all the movies you've seen in which a single villain or a group of bad guys terrorized innocent people. How does it feel to watch this kind of unchecked cruelty and evil? How does the audience respond when the hero arrives to put the evildoers in their place? How popular with moviegoers are films in which no day of reckoning awaits the bad guys?

_____

_____

_____

_____

_____

"If you do a study of all the references to the 'day of the Lord,' . . . you will find that there is a near view as well as a far view. There is a near view in terms of God's activity in the life of Israel. God was acting on planet Earth on His own behalf in the Babylonian period when He used Babylon to judge His people. He was also at work when He restored Israel from captivity during the times of the Medes and the Persians. The judgment was the Babylonian captivity. The blessing was the restoration of the remnant back into the land as recorded in Ezra, Nehemiah, Haggai, Zechariah, and Malachi. The near view was a Day of the Lord that has already been fulfilled in Israel's history.

"But there is also a far view to the Day of the Lord. That is, the Day of the Lord looks beyond the events of the Babylonian captivity and restoration to a climactic time in history that has not yet taken place. The judgment of that future day will take place during the Tribulation and at the end of the Millennium, and the blessing of that future day will be fulfilled in the earthly kingdom of Jesus, Israel's Messiah. If you want to know what the future holds, it holds a day. And that day is called the Day of the Lord." [4]

Mark Bailey

13. The Bible speaks of eventually reaping what we sow (Galatians 6:7). The message is clear: God will not be mocked or dismissed or ignored. There will be a payday. How does this truth apply to the way you read the daily newspaper? to the way you interact with neighbors?

_____

_____

_____

_____

_____

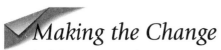

Making the Change

(*Tribulation Force,* p. 60)

Call our time "the age of man," an epoch in which rebel creatures can (and do) shove God into the shadows. But make no mistake, there is coming a "Day of the Lord"—a day belonging to him, a day in which Jesus takes center stage. Christ will no longer be viewed as an optional sideshow in life; he will be the main event. The Lamb of God will play a new role as the Lion of Judah. The baby of Bethlehem will be seen as the Judge of all the world.

[And] that day is coming quickly, as expressed in the second book of the Left Behind series:

> **THE CHURCH HAD BEEN SNATCHED AWAY**, and they had all been left behind. Bruce's message was that Jesus was coming again in what the Bible called "the glorious appearing," seven years after the beginning of the Tribulation. By then, he said, three-fourths of the world's remaining population would be wiped out, and probably a larger percentage of believers in Christ. Bruce's exhortation was not a call to be timid. It was a challenge to the convinced, to those who had been persuaded by God's most dramatic invasion of human life since the incarnation of Jesus Christ as a mortal baby.
>
> Bruce had already told the Steeles and Buck that a quarter of the earth's population would die during the second, third, and fourth judgments from the Seven-Sealed Scroll of Revelation. He cited Revelation 6:8, where the apostle John had written, "So I looked, and behold, a pale horse. And the name of him who sat on it was Death, and Hades followed with him. And power was given to them over a fourth of the earth, to kill with sword, with hunger, with death, and by the beasts of the earth."
>
> But what was to come after that was even worse.

14. Comment on Bruce's message. If you had been sitting in his audience of left behind, new believers, how would you have felt?

_____

_____

_____

_____

_____

_____

_____

15. Why should Christians not be timid in light of all that is to come?

_____

_____

_____

_____

_____

_____

16. What, if anything, is the difference between believing that Jesus is coming back and being convinced that his return is soon?

_____

_____

_____

_____

_____

_____

_____

"The time of the Tribulation is referred to in both the Old and New Testaments as 'the day of the Lord' (cf. Isaiah 13:6; 1 Thessalonians 5:2). This period is the opposite of the day of man, which is in effect today and during which God's grace limits the full expression of His wrath. But when the Day of the Lord comes, there will be no holding back His judgment." [5]

Tony Evans

Pursuing the Truth

In Genesis 18, God tells Abraham of his intention to pour out judgment on the evil cities of Sodom and Gomorrah. Abraham thinks of his relatives living in that region and is horrified at the thought of such divine wrath. He asks a very human question, "Should not the Judge of all the earth do what is right?" (18:25).

The fact is, God *does* do what is right, 100 percent of the time. He is never unjust or unfair or harsh. We can't point to a single instance in all of history in which God can be accused of having shown partiality or of having overreacted toward sin. And so when the Day of the Lord begins, as terrible as it will be for those unrepentant souls living on the earth, the fact remains that God is just, and his judgments on that day will be right.

Consider these verses from the New Living Translation:

"He will judge the world with justice and rule the nations with fairness." (Psalm 9:8)

"For the LORD is coming to judge the earth. He will judge the world with justice, and the nations with fairness." (Psalm 98:9)

"It is wrong for a judge to favor the guilty or condemn the innocent." (Proverbs 18:5)

"For there is going to come a day of judgment when God, the just judge of all the world, will judge all people according to what they have done." (Romans 2:5–6)

17. What would we conclude about God if unrepentant sinners were never held accountable for their actions?

_____

_____

_____

_____

_____

Matthew 24:21–22 says:

For that will be a time of greater horror than anything the world has ever seen or will ever see again. In fact, unless that time of calamity is shortened, the entire human race will be destroyed. But it will be shortened for the sake of God's chosen ones.

18. What does this passage reveal about the character of God?

_____

_____

_____

_____

_____

_____

19. How would you respond to someone who said: "It sounds like lots of Christians are going to suffer and die during 'the Day of the Lord.' How can God be fair or just when innocent people die as a result of his judgment?"

_____

_____

_____

_____

_____

_____

20. Describe briefly how you have been challenged by this study in each of these ways:

Motivated _____

_____

Encouraged _____

_____

Disturbed _____

_____

21. List two specific things you intend to *start* doing or *stop* doing as a result of this lesson on the Day of the Lord.

a. _____

b. _____

"No other event in the Bible, except perhaps the Second Coming itself, is mentioned more frequently than the Tribulation. It is so important that we cannot cover it all, even in the twelve books of the Left Behind series. There is no end of astonishing events from this awful period. Consider the following that are clearly described in Scripture:

1. The four horsemen of the Apocalypse (including a world war that wipes out 25 percent of the world's population)

2. The two witnesses who have the power to stop the rain and call down fire from heaven

3. The 144,000 servants of God who preach the gospel

4. A soul harvest which no one can number

5. Unprecedented martyrdom

6. Another world war that kills one-third of the world's remaining population

7. Uncounted assassinations and murders

8. Supernatural activities beyond description

No wonder Jesus said the Tribulation was unique from anything that has ever happened or would happen again!" [6]

Tim LaHaye and Jerry B. Jenkins

Lesson in Review . . .

- Shortly after the Rapture, "the Day of the Lord" will begin on the earth.
- This "day" actually includes seven years of judgment (the Tribulation) followed by the second coming of Christ and his thousand-year reign on the earth (the Millennium).
- This event demonstrates the sovereignty of God over human history and his righteousness and justice.

LEFT

BIBLE STUDY GUIDE #3

BEHIND

The Judgments

Lesson 3
Breaking the Seals

1. Have you served on a jury in a civil or criminal case? What happened?

_____

_____

_____

_____

_____

_____

_____

_____

2. What do you believe about capital punishment? Under what circumstances, if any, do you think it can be applied?

_____

_____

_____

_____

_____

_____

_____

3. Many people accuse God of being angry and vindictive. They cite the Old Testament plagues and the "doom and gloom" prophetic books (including the New Testament book of Revelation) as proof that the Lord takes pleasure in pouring out judgment on the wicked. How do you respond to this view of God?

_____

_____

_____

_____

_____

_____

Unfolding the Story

(*Tribulation Force*, pp. 29–30)

In the second book of the Left Behind series (*Tribulation Force*), pastor Bruce Barnes, himself a recent convert, gathers some new believers in Christ and they discuss what the Bible prophesies about the days to come. Notice especially what he says about the so-called "Seal Judgments."

> "**THE NEWS THAT REALLY GOT TO ME** today was the announcement that the next major order of business for Carpathia is what he calls 'an understanding' between the global community and Israel, as well as what he calls 'a special arrangement' between the U.N. and the United States."
>
> Buck sat up straighter. "What do you make of that?"
>
> "I don't know what the U.S. thing is, because as much as I study I don't see America playing a role during this period of history. But we all know what the 'understanding' with Israel will be. I don't know what form it will take or what the benefit will be to the Holy Land, but clearly this is the seven-year treaty."
>
> Chloe looked up. "And that actually signals the beginning of the seven-year period of tribulation."
>
> "Exactly." Bruce looked at the group. "If that announcement says anything about a promise from Carpathia that Israel will be protected over the next seven years, it officially ushers in the Tribulation."

Buck was taking notes. "So the disappearances, the Rapture, didn't start the seven-year period?"

"No," Bruce said. "Part of me hoped that something would delay the treaty with Israel. Nothing in Scripture says it has to happen right away. But once it does, the clock starts ticking."

"But it starts ticking toward Christ setting up his kingdom on earth, right?" Buck asked. Rayford was impressed that Buck had learned so much so quickly.

Bruce nodded. "That's right. And that's the reason for this meeting. I need to tell you all something. I am going to have a two-hour meeting, right here in this office, every weeknight from eight to ten. Just for us. . . . I can't force you to come, but I urge you. Anytime you're in town, be here. In our studies we're going to outline what God has revealed in the Scriptures. Some of it you've already heard me talk about. But if the treaty with Israel comes within the next few days, we have no time to waste. . . . Remember the seven Seal Judgments Revelation talks about? . . . Those will begin immediately, if I'm right. There will be an eighteen-month period of peace, but in the three months following that, the rest of the Seal Judgments will fall on the earth. One-fourth of the world's population will be wiped out. I don't want to be maudlin, but will you look around this room and tell me what that means to you?"

Rayford didn't have to look around the room. He sat with the three people closest to him in the world. Was it possible that in less than two years, he would lose yet another loved one?

4. What do you make of Bruce's observation that, whereas some existing countries are clearly named or alluded to in the Bible's prophetic books, America does *not* seem to be mentioned?

_____

_____

_____

_____

_____

_____

_____

_____

5. How does the promise of a coming kingdom (a thousand-year reign of Christ) *after* the great and terrible Tribulation change the way you look at these coming seven years of "hell on earth"?

_____

_____

_____

_____

_____

_____

_____

_____

6. If existing Christians will be raptured and spared the Tribulation, why wouldn't God protect post-Rapture believers in Jesus from the horrors of the Tribulation?

_____

_____

_____

_____

_____

_____

_____

_____

Back to Reality

Everybody would love to know the future (think how many TV shows and movies revolve around that idea). While we can't know every detail, we can know God's broad intentions. The Bible reveals a distinct prophetic time line—a discernible sequence of events. Following the Rapture, a series of judgments will begin to fall on the earth. This first "batch of trouble" is called the Seal Judgments.

7. Would you say most Christians (the ones that you know) read the Bible in a perfunctory, obligatory sort of way, or do they read and study it with a strong eagerness to know what God has said about what is to come? Why?

    _____

    _____

    _____

    _____

    _____

    _____

    _____

8. The Bible speaks of the "fear of the Lord." Previous generations of Christians strongly emphasized this concept; modern Christians don't so much. Why?

    _____

    _____

    _____

    _____

    _____

    _____

The Fear of the Lord

What does the Bible mean when it makes statements like these?

"Fear of the LORD is a life-giving fountain; it offers escape from the snares of death." (Proverbs 14:27)

"Fear of the LORD gives life, security, and protection from harm." (Proverbs 19:23)

"The church then had peace throughout Judea, Galilee, and Samaria, and it grew in strength and numbers. The believers were walking in the fear of the Lord and in the comfort of the Holy Spirit." (Acts 9:31)

"It is because we know this solemn fear of the Lord that we work so hard to persuade others. God knows we are sincere, and I hope you know this, too." (2 Corinthians 5:11)

The type of *fear* referred to in verses like these connotes a sense of awe. Contrary to widespread belief, it does not mean a cowering kind of dread or terror. Rather, to fear the Lord implies reverence or respect for God. He is our almighty Creator, perfect in holiness and judgment. Because he is high and lifted up, we do not treat him with contempt. We do not come before him lightly or glibly. We must never assume that we control him, that he exists for our pleasure, or to do our bidding. On the contrary, we must recognize that we were created by him and for him. So we approach him with deep humility and gratitude, recognizing both his greatness and his grace. And when we fear him rightly, we fear nothing else.

9. There was a time in our culture when even irreligious people maintained a certain respect for the Creator. Now it is acceptable to say anything about God and his people. Why do you think there has been such a change in attitude toward God?

_____

_____

_____

_____

_____

_____

_____

Understanding the Word

The seven Seal Judgments mentioned in the Left Behind novels are not fictitious plot devices. They are revealed clearly in Revelation 6:1–17:

> As I watched, the Lamb broke the first of the seven seals on the scroll. Then one of the four living beings called out with a voice that sounded like thunder, "Come!" I looked up and saw a white horse. Its rider carried a bow, and a crown was placed on his head. He rode out to win many battles and gain the victory.
>
> When the Lamb broke the second seal, I heard the second living being say, "Come!" And another horse appeared, a red one. Its rider was given a mighty sword and the authority to remove peace from the earth. And there was war and slaughter everywhere.
>
> When the Lamb broke the third seal, I heard the third living being say, "Come!" And I looked up and saw a black horse, and its rider was holding a pair of scales in his hand. And a voice from among the four living beings said, "A loaf of wheat bread or three loaves of barley for a day's pay. And don't waste the olive oil and wine."

And when the Lamb broke the fourth seal, I heard the fourth living being say, "Come!" And I looked up and saw a horse whose color was pale green like a corpse. And Death was the name of its rider, who was followed around by the Grave. They were given authority over one-fourth of the earth, to kill with the sword and famine and disease and wild animals.

And when the Lamb broke the fifth seal, I saw under the altar the souls of all who had been martyred for the word of God and for being faithful in their witness. They called loudly to the Lord and said, "O Sovereign Lord, holy and true, how long will it be before you judge the people who belong to this world for what they have done to us? When will you avenge our blood against these people?" Then a white robe was given to each of them. And they were told to rest a little longer until the full number of their brothers and sisters—their fellow servants of Jesus—had been martyred.

I watched as the Lamb broke the sixth seal, and there was a great earthquake. The sun became as dark as black cloth, and the moon became as red as blood. Then the stars of the sky fell to the earth like green figs falling from trees shaken by mighty winds. And the sky was rolled up like a scroll and taken away. And all of the mountains and all of the islands disappeared. Then the kings of the earth, the rulers, the generals, the wealthy people, the people with great power, and every slave and every free person—all hid themselves in the caves and among the rocks of the mountains. And they cried to the mountains and the rocks, "Fall on us and hide us from the face of the one who sits on the throne and from the wrath of the Lamb. For the great day of their wrath has come, and who will be able to survive?"

10. Who does John see breaking these seals and unleashing these judgments on the earth? Who does that figure represent?

_____

_____

_____

_____

_____

_____

_____

_____

_____

11. Revelation 6:1–8 depicts the famous "Four Horsemen of the Apocalypse." What judgments do each of these horse and riders bring?

Example: the white horse = Antichrist

the red horse = _____

the black horse = _____

the pale horse = _____

"The color of the fourth horse is 'pale,' or better, 'yellowish-green.' . . . This one alone among the four horsemen is named, and he is called Death. . . . The effect of this judgment is that one-fourth of the population of earth is killed. . . . The means of extermination are four: sword (war), hunger (famine that often follows war), death (perhaps by plagues of diseases which often accompany war) and wild beasts of the earth (which apparently will be unrestrained and will roam to kill men). Suddenly all of man's programs for bringing in peace, plenty and longevity through medicine will be overturned in the short time that it will take to accompany this judgment." [1]

Charles Ryrie

---

12. According to the passage above, what will happen when the fifth and sixth seals are broken?

_____

_____

_____

_____

_____

_____

Finding the Connection

The Left Behind books offer a chilling look at these terrible Seal Judgments. The fifth seal is especially hard for many Christians to understand. It relates to those Tribulation saints who will be brutally killed by the forces of Antichrist because of their allegiance to Christ.

To Western Christians this kind of religious persecution is almost unthinkable. And yet it goes on all the time. In fact, according to some watchdog groups, *more Christians were mar-*

tyred for their faith in the twentieth century than in the previous nineteen centuries combined! Unfortunately, we don't often hear about these atrocities and persecutions unless they involve Western missionaries.

Clearly the forces of evil are building in their vicious hatred for God and the people of God. Every indication is that things on earth are coming to a head. Facts like these lead one to conclude that we just may be closer to the events of the Left Behind novels than most people assume.

The fifth Seal Judgment—the martyrdom of Tribulation believers—is described in these terms:

> And when the Lamb broke the fifth seal, I saw under the altar the souls of all who had been martyred for the word of God and for being faithful in their witness. They called loudly to the Lord and said, "O Sovereign Lord, holy and true, how long will it be before you judge the people who belong to this world for what they have done to us? When will you avenge our blood against these people?" Then a white robe was given to each of them. And they were told to rest a little longer until the full number of their brothers and sisters—their fellow servants of Jesus—had been martyred. (Revelation 6:9–11)

13. How does this "window into heaven" reveal God's mercy? his sovereignty (i.e., control of events)?

_____

_____

_____

_____

_____

_____

14. What do you think would have to happen for even Christians living in countries with freedom of religious expression to face overt persecution for their faith?

_____

_____

_____

_____

_____

15. How would you react/respond if the "religious climate" suddenly turned nasty where you live, and practicing your faith put your very life on the line?

_____

_____

_____

_____

_____

_____

_____

"One man who heard about these . . . seals was so impressed with the possibility of the soon second coming of the Lord that he said, 'I sometimes think I hear the hoofbeats of the four horsemen of the Apocalypse.' I replied, 'Don't listen for hoofbeats, because the shout of the Savior from heaven to call His church to be with Himself comes first!' It can't be far off!" [2]

Tim LaHaye and Jerry B. Jenkins

Making the Change
(*Tribulation Force*, p. 432)

If you *are* a follower of Jesus, you do not have to fear the Seal Judgments. Those worldwide catastrophes will come during the Tribulation period, *after* the Rapture of all Christians. If you are *not* a believer in Christ, consider this scene from the lives of those living on earth after the Rapture.

Bruce's explanation of the seventh seal made it clear that it was still a mystery even to him.

THE SEVENTH SEAL IS SO AWESOME that when it is revealed in heaven, there is silence for half an hour. It seems to progress from the sixth seal, the greatest earthquake in history, and serves to initiate the seven Trumpet Judgments, which, of course, are progressively worse than the Seal Judgments.

Amanda tried to summarize for Rayford: "We're looking at a world war, famine, plagues, death, the martyrdom of the saints, an earthquake, and then silence in heaven as the world is readied for the next seven judgments."

Rayford shook his head, then cast his eyes down. "Bruce has been warning us of this all along. There are times I think I'm ready for whatever comes and other times when I wish the end would simply come quickly."

"This is the price we pay," she said, "for ignoring the warnings when we had the chance."

16. How do you feel after reading that passage? How does it motivate you?

_____

_____

_____

_____

_____

_____

17. What are some of the specific ways you feel God has warned you about things in your life? What have you done about these warnings?

_____

_____

_____

_____

_____

18. Why is it important for Christians to realize that the universe is not out of control, and that even terrible future events like the Seal Judgments are within the plans and purposes of God?

_____

_____

_____

_____

_____

_____

Pursuing the Truth

Following the breaking of the sixth seal, we are given a peek into heaven itself. Carefully read this passage:

> Then I saw four angels standing at the four corners of the earth, holding back the four winds from blowing upon the earth. Not a leaf rustled in the trees, and the sea became as smooth as glass. And I saw another angel coming from the east, carrying the seal of the living God. And he shouted out to those four angels who had been given power to injure land and sea, "Wait! Don't hurt the land or the sea or the trees until we have placed the seal of God on the foreheads of his servants."
>
> And I heard how many were marked with the seal of God. There were 144,000 who were sealed from all the tribes of Israel: from Judah 12,000; from Reuben 12,000; from Gad 12,000; from Asher 12,000; from Naphtali 12,000; from Manasseh 12,000; from Simeon 12,000; from Levi 12,000; from Issachar 12,000; from Zebulun 12,000; from Joseph 12,000; from Benjamin 12,000.
>
> After this I saw a vast crowd, too great to count, from every nation and tribe and people and language, standing in front of the throne and before the Lamb. They were clothed in white and held palm branches in their hands. And they were shouting with a mighty shout, "Salvation comes from our God on the throne and from the Lamb!"
>
> And all the angels were standing around the throne and around the elders and the four living beings. And they fell face down before the throne and worshiped God. They said, "Amen! Blessing and glory and wisdom and thanksgiving and honor and power and strength belong to our God forever and forever. Amen!"
>
> Then one of the twenty-four elders asked me, "Who are these who are clothed in white? Where do they come from?"
>
> And I said to him, "Sir, you are the one who knows."
>
> Then he said to me, "These are the ones coming out of the great tribulation. They washed their robes in the blood of the Lamb and made them white. That is why they are standing in front of the throne of God, serving him day and night in his Temple. And he who sits on the throne will live among them and shelter them. They will never again be hungry or thirsty, and they will be fully protected from the scorching noontime heat. For the Lamb who stands in front of the throne will be their Shepherd. He will lead them to the springs of life-giving water. And God will wipe away all their tears." (Revelation 7:1–17)

19. What does this passage say about

    people trusting Christ during the Tribulation? _____

    _____

    the character of God? _____

    _____

    the power of God? _____

    _____

    the mood in heaven? _____

    _____

Read the following statement—a promise, if you will—from the pen of the apostle Paul.

> *Yes, and everyone who wants to live a godly life in Christ Jesus will suffer persecution.*
> (2 Timothy 3:12)

20. Has suffering persecution been part of your experience? If not, why do you think? What does that mean?

    _____

    _____

    _____

    _____

    _____

21. We tend to think of Jesus as a "meek and mild" Savior—perhaps even a namby-pamby Messiah. How does what you've seen in this lesson, together with the following verses from the Gospels, alter that image of Christ? Write a brief descriptive sentence about Jesus based on each of the verses.

> *Do not suppose that I have come to bring peace to the earth. I did not come to bring peace, but a sword. For I have come to turn "a man against his father, a daughter against her mother, a daughter-in-law against her mother-in-law."* (Matthew 10:34–35 NIV)

    _____

    _____

I have come to bring fire on the earth, and how I wish it were already kindled! . . . Do you think I came to bring peace on earth? No, I tell you, but division. (Luke 12:49, 51 NIV)

_____

_____

Jesus said, "For judgment I have come into this world, so that the blind will see and those who see will become blind." (John 9:39 NIV)

_____

_____

22. Summarize what you've learned in this study of the Seal Judgments. Name one "action step" you intend to take as a result:

_____

_____

_____

_____

_____

"How shall we then live? How shall we respond to what is happening around us? We should be light. And what does light do? Light exposes darkness. Light symbolizes the presence of God. Light represents all that is good. God is calling each of us to be a light-bearer. In our homes. In our churches. In our communities. In our places of work. God wants us to recognize that we are not of the darkness; we are of the light." [3]

Larry Mercer

Lesson in Review . . .

- Sometime after the Antichrist signs a peace treaty with Israel following the Rapture, the Tribulation will officially begin.
- The first great series of judgments during the Tribulation are the so-called Seal Judgments described in Revelation 6–7.
- Because of war, famine, disease, and natural catastrophes, hundreds of millions of people will die, including a large number of Tribulation saints who will be martyred for their unwavering faith in Jesus.

LEFT
BIBLE STUDY GUIDE #3
BEHIND

The Judgments

Lesson 4
Blowing the Trumpets

1. Have you ever experienced a frightening natural disaster? What happened?

_____

_____

_____

_____

_____

_____

2. How did you feel and what did you think as you observed the events of the 2003 war in Iraq?

_____

_____

_____

_____

_____

3. In what ways were your responses to that war the same and different than your response to the loss of the space shuttle Columbia?

_____

_____

_____

_____

Unfolding the Story

(*Soul Harvest*, pp. 407–12)

So far in this study guide we have looked at the truth that our merciful and loving Lord is also the righteous Judge of the universe (lesson one), and the day is coming when he will set everything right with perfect justice. That "day" of justice (see lesson 2) is actually a long period of time beginning with the seven-year Tribulation and including the Second Coming and the thousand-year millennial rule of Christ. In lesson 3, we studied the first series of worldwide judgments that will occur during the Tribulation, the Seal Judgments.

Now we turn our attention to the second set of judgments foretold in the book of Revelation, called the Trumpet Judgments. Here's a scene from *Soul Harvest*, the fourth book in the Left Behind series:

> **THE SKY GREW BLACK,** and the hailstones got bigger. Only slightly smaller than golf balls now, they rattled against the roof, clanged off the downspouts, thundered on the Range Rover, and the power failed. . . . As they watched, the sky lit up. But it wasn't lightning. The hailstones, at least half of them, were in flames!
>
> "Oh, dear ones!" Tsion said. "You know what this is, do you not? . . . The angel of the first Trumpet Judgment is throwing hail and fire to the earth. . . .
>
> Huge hailstones plopped into the river and floated downstream. They accumulated on the bank and turned the sand white like snow. Snow in the desert. Flaming darts sizzled and hissed as they hit the water. . . . Mac suddenly unclipped his belt and leaned forward. "What is that, Ray? It's raining, but it's red! Look at that! All over the snow!"
>
> "It's blood," Rayford said, a peace flooding over his soul. It did not assuage his grief, . . . but this show, this shower of fire and ice and blood, reminded him yet again that God is faithful. He keeps his promises. While our ways are not his ways and we can never understand him this side of heaven, Rayford was assured again that he was on the side of the army that had already won this war. . . .
>
> As the clouds faded and the sun returned, the results of the light show became obvious. The bark on the trees had been blackened, the foliage all burned off. As the hail melted and blood seeped into the ground, the charred grass showed through.
>
> "The Scriptures told us that one-third of the trees and all of the green grass in the world would be burned," Tsion said.

4. Hail is one thing, but *large flaming hailstones* are another! How do you think people would respond to such a phenomenon? How could something like this *not* prompt people to turn to God?

_____

_____

_____

_____

_____

5. Why did Rayford feel peace and not terror when blood began raining from the sky?

_____

_____

_____

_____

_____

Back to Reality

Is the scene above just creative fiction or some apocalyptic wishful thinking? If you take the Bible at face value, these earth-shattering events are an imminent reality. Pondering them ought to make our hearts race and our minds spin. As the old country preacher used to say, "If this don't ring your bell, your clapper's broke!" Judgment *is* coming. The world is winding down. The great showdown between good and evil is just ahead.

6. How, if at all, has your reading of the Left Behind books and your study of these lessons changed you? What is different in your attitudes? Your actions?

_____

_____

_____

_____

7. Why would it be in the enemy's interest to keep people ignorant or skeptical of these Bible truths?

    _____

    _____

    _____

    _____

    _____

    _____

8. If Christians were genuinely convinced of the imminent return of Christ and the fleeting future of this present world, how would it alter the way we live in a typical day?

    _____

    _____

    _____

    _____

    _____

"While the seal judgments occur in roughly the first twenty-one months of the Tribulation, the trumpet judgments take place in the second twenty-one months. In the first period of the Tribulation the earth has known the wrath of the Antichrist; now it will begin to feel the wrath of God Almighty." [1]

                                                             Tim LaHaye and Jerry B. Jenkins

---

Understanding the Word

Following the Seal Judgments of Revelation 6 come the Trumpet Judgments of Revelation 8–9. Here is what God revealed to the apostle John (and, ultimately, to us):

> Then the seven angels with the seven trumpets prepared to blow their mighty blasts. The first angel blew his trumpet, and hail and fire mixed with blood were thrown down upon the earth, and one-third of the earth was set on fire. One-third of the trees were burned, and all the grass was burned.

Then the second angel blew his trumpet, and a great mountain of fire was thrown into the sea. And one-third of the water in the sea became blood. And one-third of all things living in the sea died. And one-third of all the ships on the sea were destroyed.

Then the third angel blew his trumpet, and a great flaming star fell out of the sky, burning like a torch. It fell upon one-third of the rivers and on the springs of water. The name of the star was Bitterness. It made one-third of the water bitter, and many people died because the water was so bitter.

Then the fourth angel blew his trumpet, and one-third of the sun was struck, and one-third of the moon, and one-third of the stars, and they became dark. And one-third of the day was dark and one-third of the night also.

Then I looked up. And I heard a single eagle crying loudly as it flew through the air, "Terror, terror, terror to all who belong to this world because of what will happen when the last three angels blow their trumpets." (Revelation 8:6–13)

9. What will happen to the earth's vegetation as a result of the first Trumpet Judgment? What might be some of the worldwide implications of losing one-third of the earth's vegetation?

_____

_____

_____

_____

_____

10. How do the second and third Trumpet Judgments affect the earth's waters?

_____

_____

_____

_____

WHAT IF . . . an enormous meteorite crashed into one of the earth's oceans and a third of the sea became blood?

"You don't have to be a scientist to see how such a cataclysm would cause unprecedented tidal waves. Would this comet contain heavy radioactivity? Imagine hundreds—perhaps even thousands—of overturned oil tankers and ships filled with toxic waste. Ponder countless seaside chemical and nuclear plants breaking apart and spilling their poisons into swollen bays and inland rivers? Clearly such a disaster would radically alter the entire ecosystem of the earth.

"Consider also that the World Health Organization says that 'nearly half of the world's people are affected by diseases related to insufficient and contaminated water,' which is why the WHO is trying to improve the water supplies of the world. We shudder to think of the plagues that will be spread when the water supply turns bitter, then to blood in that 'great and terrible Day of the Lord.' " [2]

Tim LaHaye and Jerry B. Jenkins

11. The biblical passages about the Trumpet Judgments provoke some interesting footnotes and insights. Some translations of the Bible give the name of the fallen star of Revelation 8:11 as "Wormwood." The New Living Translation calls it "Bitterness." What is the significance of this name?

_____

_____

_____

_____

_____

"Many species of wormwood grow in Palestine, and all have a strong, bitter (but not poisonous) taste, which causes the plant to be used as a symbol of bitterness, sorrow, and calamity. This plague [described in Revelation 8:10–11] will make a third part of the fresh water supply of the earth unfit for human consumption." [3]

Charles Ryrie

12. What are the practical implications of total darkness descending on the earth? (For example, think about an experience you have had in complete darkness.)

_____

_____

_____

_____

_____

_____

The Trumpet Judgments continue in Revelation 9:

Then the fifth angel blew his trumpet, and I saw a star that had fallen to earth from the sky, and he was given the key to the shaft of the bottomless pit. When he opened it, smoke poured out as though from a huge furnace, and the sunlight and air were darkened by the smoke.

Then locusts came from the smoke and descended on the earth, and they were given power to sting like scorpions. They were told not to hurt the grass or plants or trees but to attack all the people who did not have the seal of God on their foreheads. They were told not to kill them but to torture them for five months with agony like the pain of scorpion stings. In those days people will seek death but will not find it. They will long to die, but death will flee away!

The locusts looked like horses armed for battle. They had gold crowns on their heads, and they had human faces. Their hair was long like the hair of a woman, and their teeth were like the teeth of a lion. They wore armor made of iron, and their wings roared like an army of chariots rushing into battle. They had tails that stung like scorpions, with power to torture people. This power was given to them for five months. Their king is the angel from the bottomless pit; his name in Hebrew is Abaddon, and in Greek, Apollyon—the Destroyer.

The first terror is past, but look, two more terrors are coming!

Then the sixth angel blew his trumpet, and I heard a voice speaking from the four horns of the gold altar that stands in the presence of God. And the voice spoke to the sixth angel who held the trumpet: "Release the four angels who are bound at the great Euphrates River." And the four angels who had been prepared for this hour and day and month and year were turned loose to kill one-third of all the people on earth. They led an army of 200 million mounted troops—I heard an announcement of how many there were.

And in my vision, I saw the horses and the riders sitting on them. The riders wore armor that was fiery red and sky blue and yellow. The horses' heads were like the heads of lions, and fire and smoke and burning sulfur billowed from their mouths. One-third of all the people on earth were killed by these three plagues—by the fire and the smoke and burning sulfur that came from the mouths of the horses. Their power was in their mouths, but also in their tails. For their tails had heads like snakes, with the power to injure people.

But the people who did not die in these plagues still refused to turn from their evil deeds. They continued to worship demons and idols made of gold, silver, bronze, stone, and wood—idols that neither see nor hear nor walk! And they did not repent of their murders or their witchcraft or their immorality or their thefts. (Revelation 9:1–21)

13. The fifth Trumpet Judgment releases an army of locusts. How are they described?

_____

_____

_____

_____

_____

Locusts or Scorpions?

"Victims of scorpion bites say the animal's venom seems to set one's veins and nervous system on fire, but the pain is gone after a few days; not so with these locusts. They are given power to torment 'those men who do not have the seal of God on their foreheads' for five long months. Yet unlike normal locusts, these beasts attack only unregenerate human beings, never foliage. . . .

"This seems to be one of the plagues that God sends on the followers of Antichrist to hinder them from proselytizing among the uncommitted of the world. It may also give Tribulation saints some time to prepare themselves for the soon-to-come Great Tribulation."[4]

Tim LaHaye and Jerry B. Jenkins

Lest we be tempted to think that the Trumpet Judgments and other examples of God's wrath are simply poured out on the earth, it is important to remember that God never ceases to be in control of his creation. As Charles Ryrie reminds us, "Although this judgment is literally hell on earth, the overruling power of God is interwoven throughout this passage. He allows this judgment to occur; He sets the limits on the destructive power of these locusts; He brings it to a conclusion when His purpose in it is finished. He is in complete control."[5]

14. What clues in the description of the horsemen of the sixth Trumpet Judgment tell you they may be demonic/supernatural in nature and not, as many have speculated, an invading army of humans from the East?

_____

_____

_____

_____

_____

Finding the Connection

Both the Bible and the Left Behind books depict two kinds of people during the earth's final days. First are those people who acknowledge the reality, power, holiness, and mercy of God. In humility, repentance, and faith, these souls turn to God and ask for forgiveness. Second are those people who see all these things and yet foolishly harden their hearts and run *away* from God, crying out "to the mountains and the rocks, 'Fall on us and hide us from the face of the one who sits on the throne and from the wrath of the Lamb. For the great day of their wrath has come, and who will be able to survive?'" (Revelation 6:16–17).

15. How do you account for these varying reactions? (Hint: see 2 Corinthians 4:4.)

_____

_____

_____

_____

_____

16. In what ways do you see this kind of divergent response today, even before the Rapture and the Tribulation?

_____

_____

_____

_____

17. How do the Seal Judgments (that will occur in the first twenty-one months of the Tribulation) compare and contrast with the Trumpet Judgments (that will occur in the second twenty-one months of the Tribulation)?

_____

_____

_____

_____

Making the Change

(*Soul Harvest*, pp. 417–19)

For most Christians the problem isn't that we don't know what to do. The problem is that we often don't do what we know. James 4:17 warns: "Remember, it is sin to know what you ought to do and then not do it."

Consider how the Left Behind believers responded when they began experiencing the events of the Trumpet Judgments:

> NEWSCASTERS TOLD THE STORY of what astronomers had discovered only two hours before—a brand-new comet on a collision course with the Earth. . . . "Ladies and Gentlemen, I urge you to put this in perspective. This object is about to enter Earth's atmosphere. Scientists have not determined its makeup, but if—as it appears—it is less dense than granite, the friction resulting from entry will make it burst into flames.
>
> "Once subject to Earth's gravitational pull, it will accelerate at thirty-two feet per second squared. As you can see from these pictures, it is immense. But until you realize its size, you cannot fathom the potential destruction on the way. GC astronomers estimate it at no less than the mass of the entire Appalachian Mountain range. It has the potential to split the earth or to knock it from its orbit.
>
> "The Global Community Aeronautics and Space Administration projects the collision at approximately 9:00 A.M., Central Standard Time. They anticipate the best possible scenario, that it will take place in the middle of the Atlantic Ocean.
>
> "Tidal waves are expected to engulf coasts on both sides of the Atlantic for up to fifty miles inland. Coastal areas are being evacuated as we speak. Crews of ocean-going vessels are being plucked from their ships by helicopters, though it is unknown how many can be moved to safety in time. Experts agree the impact on marine life will be inestimable. . . ."

The Tribulation Force went to their computers to spread the word that this was the second Trumpet Judgment foretold in Revelation 8:8–9. "Will we look like expert prognosticators when the results are in?" Tsion wrote. "Will it shock the powers that be to discover that, just as the Bible says, one-third of the fish will die and one-third of the ships at sea will sink, and tidal waves will wreak havoc on the entire world? Or will officials reinterpret the events to make it appear the Bible was wrong? Do not be fooled! Do not delay! Now is the accepted time. Now is the day of salvation. Come to Christ before it is too late. Things will only get worse. We were all left behind the first time. Do not be left behind when you breathe your last."

18. How did the approaching comet motivate the members of the Tribulation Force?

_____

_____

_____

_____

_____

19. Discuss how can you apply the following statement of Jesus to the way you pray for others: *"For people can't come to me unless the Father who sent me draws them to me"* (John 6:44).

_____

_____

_____

_____

_____

Pursuing the Truth

If you are still troubled by the fact that God would allow believers to suffer through the Tribulation judgments and use the Antichrist to bring judgment on the earth through the Seal Judgments, read the short Old Testament book of Habakkuk. There the prophet was horrified that God would use the Babylonians to judge the rebellious nation of Judah. Yet by the end of the book, Habakkuk was once again trusting in the wisdom and purposes of God:

I trembled inside when I heard all this; my lips quivered with fear. My legs gave way beneath me, and I shook in terror. I will wait quietly for the coming day when disaster will strike the people who invade us. Even though the fig trees have no blossoms, and there are no grapes on the vine; even though the olive crop fails, and the fields lie empty and barren; even though the flocks die in the fields, and the cattle barns are empty, yet I will rejoice in the LORD! I will be joyful in the God of my salvation. The Sovereign LORD is my strength! He will make me as surefooted as a deer and bring me safely over the mountains. (Habakkuk 3:16–19)

20. In what way does Habakkuk's response encourage you?

_____

_____

_____

_____

_____

_____

21. Another instance of God's judgment is found in Exodus 10. How does the fourth Trumpet Judgment (darkness on the earth) compare with God's last two plagues on the Egyptians?

_____

_____

_____

_____

_____

_____

_____

Notice what happens with the blowing of the seventh trumpet. It doesn't really result in a judgment, so much as it shows heaven celebrating the imminent, ultimate victory of Christ over the Antichrist:

Then the seventh angel blew his trumpet, and there were loud voices shouting in heaven: "The whole world has now become the kingdom of our Lord and of his Christ, and he will reign forever and ever."

And the twenty-four elders sitting on their thrones before God fell on their faces and worshiped him. And they said,

"We give thanks to you, Lord God Almighty, the one who is and who always was, for now you have assumed your great power and have begun to reign. The nations were angry with you, but now the time of your wrath has come. It is time to judge the dead and reward your servants. You will reward your prophets and your holy people, all who fear your name, from the least to the greatest. And you will destroy all who have caused destruction on the earth."

Then, in heaven, the Temple of God was opened and the Ark of his covenant could be seen inside the Temple. Lightning flashed, thunder crashed and roared; there was a great hailstorm, and the world was shaken by a mighty earthquake. (Revelation 11:15–19)

22. What does this passage tell you about the purpose of the seventh trumpet? How does this encourage you?

_____

_____

_____

_____

_____

_____

_____

"You might think that when all the horrors prophesied in the Bible begin unfolding on earth, people would run to God crying for mercy and salvation. You'd think that once people realize they are in the last days of God's judgment, and they see all these terrifying things unfolding before their eyes, they would repent and beg God's forgiveness.

"Not so. According to Revelation 9:20–21, 'The rest of mankind, who were not killed by these plagues, did not repent of the works of their hands.' . . . God is warning the world today to repent or feel His wrath to come. The day of His grace is still upon us, and whoever will may come to the Cross and find forgiveness. But when the day of God's judgment falls, sinners will not be inclined to seek forgiveness. Don't let anyone you know be left behind to face the blast of God's judgment." [7]

Tony Evans

Lesson in Review . . .

- The seventh Seal Judgment of the Tribulation will usher in a series of seven Trumpet Judgments.
- These Trumpet Judgments will be far more terrible than the Seal Judgments, but a great many people will still refuse to turn to God.
- Because of the judgments to come, Christians need to be praying for family members, friends, neighbors, and colleagues who do not know Christ. And just as importantly, we need to ask God for opportunities to share the love of Christ with them.

The Judgments

Lesson 5
The Overturned Bowls

1. As a get-acquainted exercise, answer the following questions:
   - Do you like seafood? If so, what is your favorite kind? _____
   - What is your favorite drink when you are *really* thirsty? _____
   - Are you afraid of the dark? _____
   - Do you prefer the heat of summer or the cold of winter? _____
   - Are you a person who likes to get a tan at the beach or pool? _____

   (NOTE: You *will* see the connection between these questions and the rest of this study by the time we are done!)

Unfolding the Story
(*Desecration*, pp. 110–11)

This lesson will look at the so-called Bowl Judgments (or "vial judgments") of the Great Tribulation. Following the Seal Judgments and the Trumpet Judgments, God will unleash a series of even more catastrophic punishments on our rebellious planet. Here's how these events are introduced in the Left Behind series:

> "THEY ARE SUFFERING. . . . They received the mark of the beast; then they worshiped his image. And now they are victims of Revelation 16:1–2."
>
> "The plague of boils!" Buck whispered.
>
> Chaim looked at him meaningfully with a close-mouthed smile, then moved away from Buck and into an open area. Buck stumbled and nearly toppled, startled by the huge, deep sounds emitting from the little man's throat. Chaim's voice was so loud that everyone stopped and stared, and Buck had to cover his ears.

"I heard a great voice out of the temple!" Chaim shouted, "saying to the seven angels, 'Go your ways, and pour out the bowls of the wrath of God upon the earth.' And the first went, and poured out his bowl upon the earth; and there fell a noisome and grievous sore upon the men which had the mark of the beast, and upon them which worshiped his image."

The thousands who had been milling about fell back at the piercing voice, and Buck was astounded at Chaim's bearing. He stood straighter and looked taller, his chest puffed out as he inhaled between sentences. His eyes were ablaze, his jaw set, and he gestured with balled fists.

2. According to Chaim, what people will fall victim to this future plague of boils?

_____
_____
_____
_____
_____

3. What do you think happened to give Chaim such power and boldness in this scene?

_____
_____
_____
_____
_____

"These judgments, when compared to the seal and trumpet judgments, appear to be the most intense and severe. It appears that these bowls have been collecting God's wrath, so to speak, for a long time. Now they are filled to the brim and ready to be poured, which will prepare the way for Christ's second coming. The angels who administer these judgments are pictured as turning the bowls upside down to ensure that every last drop of God's wrath goes forth. . . . Nothing is held back." [1]

Tim LaHaye and Thomas Ice

Back to Reality

Thanks to the growing influence of video games and an overabundance of Hollywood special effects, the lines between fantasy and reality in our culture have become quite blurry. Couple this with "real-time" camera shots taking us visually into the middle of war and tragedy while we remain in the comfortable surroundings of our homes, and you can see why we are jaded. In truth, genuine awe is nearly a lost sensation.

Most people don't have a clue that the Bible talks matter-of-factly and explicitly about earth's last days. And many of those who *do* happen to read the Bible's preview of end-times events do so without even batting an eye. After all, when you've just seen the handsome hero of Tinseltown's latest disaster flick save the world, destroy the bad guys, and get the girl—all in under two hours—it's tough to be impressed by some cryptic documents written thousands of years ago!

All the more reason to turn off the tube and pick up the Scriptures. It is there and there alone that we find a stunning outline for the end of the world as we know it.

4. Before reading the Left Behind books and/or participating in this Bible study, what was your basic understanding of end-times events? From what sources did you get your information? On what ideas did you base your opinions?

    _____

    _____

    _____

    _____

    _____

    _____

5. Is it hard for you to get excited or to feel awe, especially about the promises or prophecies of God? Why or why not?

    _____

    _____

    _____

    _____

    _____

6. In what ways does this study of the earth's last days prompt you to look at current world events in a different light?

_____

_____

_____

_____

Understanding the Word

The great judgments decreed for the world after the Rapture and before the Second Coming of Christ should not be lightly dismissed. Here is what the book of Revelation says about the Bowl Judgments that will be poured out on the earth just after the midpoint of the seven-year Tribulation period:

> Then I heard a mighty voice shouting from the Temple to the seven angels, "Now go your ways and empty out the seven bowls of God's wrath on the earth."
>
> So the first angel left the Temple and poured out his bowl over the earth, and horrible, malignant sores broke out on everyone who had the mark of the beast and who worshiped his statue.
>
> Then the second angel poured out his bowl on the sea, and it became like the blood of a corpse. And everything in the sea died.
>
> Then the third angel poured out his bowl on the rivers and springs, and they became blood. And I heard the angel who had authority over all water saying, "You are just in sending this judgment, O Holy One, who is and who always was. For your holy people and your prophets have been killed, and their blood was poured out on the earth. So you have given their murderers blood to drink. It is their just reward." And I heard a voice from the altar saying, "Yes, Lord God Almighty, your punishments are true and just."
>
> Then the fourth angel poured out his bowl on the sun, causing it to scorch everyone with its fire. Everyone was burned by this blast of heat, and they cursed the name of God, who sent all of these plagues. They did not repent and give him glory.
>
> Then the fifth angel poured out his bowl on the throne of the beast, and his kingdom was plunged into darkness. And his subjects ground their teeth in anguish, and they cursed the God of heaven for their pains and sores. But they refused to repent of all their evil deeds.
>
> Then the sixth angel poured out his bowl on the great Euphrates River, and it dried up

so that the kings from the east could march their armies westward without hindrance. And I saw three evil spirits that looked like frogs leap from the mouth of the dragon, the beast, and the false prophet. These miracle-working demons caused all the rulers of the world to gather for battle against the Lord on that great judgment day of God Almighty.

"Take note: I will come as unexpectedly as a thief! Blessed are all who are watching for me, who keep their robes ready so they will not need to walk naked and ashamed."

And they gathered all the rulers and their armies to a place called Armageddon in Hebrew.

Then the seventh angel poured out his bowl into the air. And a mighty shout came from the throne of the Temple in heaven, saying, "It is finished!" Then the thunder crashed and rolled, and lightning flashed. And there was an earthquake greater than ever before in human history. The great city of Babylon split into three pieces, and cities around the world fell into heaps of rubble. And so God remembered all of Babylon's sins, and he made her drink the cup that was filled with the wine of his fierce wrath. And every island disappeared, and all the mountains were leveled. There was a terrible hailstorm, and hailstones weighing seventy-five pounds fell from the sky onto the people below. They cursed God because of the hailstorm, which was a very terrible plague. (Revelation 16:1–2)

7. Spend a few minutes summarizing the effects of each of the seven Bowl Judgments mentioned in Revelation 16:

   a. The first bowl (16:2) _____

   _____

   _____

   b. The second bowl (16:3) _____

   _____

   _____

"Everything in the sea died."

"The rather vivid phrase pictures ships wallowing in blood. Under the second trumpet judgment, a third of the sea creatures die (8:9); now the destruction of marine life will be total. Can you imagine the stench and disease this will bring to people who live along the seashores of the world? Seventy-two percent of earth's surface is water."[2]

Charles Ryrie

c. The third bowl (16:4) _____

_____

_____

"By this point in the Tribulation the Antichrist and his forces have martyred millions of believers. Therefore God seems to say to him, 'You like blood? Very well. Then you may have it to drink!' Is this literal blood? Who knows for sure? But if Jesus could turn water into wine at the marriage feast of Cana, surely He would have no problems turning water into blood. Whatever the case, because of its rebellious, murderous ways, the world will find itself without drinking water. And so the prayer of the martyred saints in Revelation 6:10 will be abundantly answered. They asked, 'How long, O Lord, holy and true, until You judge and avenge our blood on those who dwell on the earth?' This plague of blood is God's answer."[3]

Tim LaHaye and Jerry B. Jenkins

---

d. The fourth bowl (16:8–9) _____

_____

_____

e. The fifth bowl (16:10–11) _____

_____

_____

f. The sixth bowl (16:12–16) _____

_____

_____

g. The seventh bowl (16:17–21) _____

_____

_____

8. After pouring out the third bowl of judgment, why does the angel say the punishment of blood is their "just reward"?

_____

_____

_____

_____

_____

9. Why is the fourth Bowl Judgment especially excruciating in light of the second and third bowls?

_____

_____

_____

_____

10. How will the people of earth respond to each of these judgments?

_____

_____

_____

_____

11. How can people witness undeniable miracles firsthand and still refuse to humble themselves before God?

_____

_____

_____

_____

Finding the Connection

It is interesting to compare the ten plagues of Egypt with the seven Bowl Judgments of the Great Tribulation. Look at the lists that follow and note the similarities.

The Plagues of Egypt
(Exodus 7–11)

Nile turns to blood   Gnats (or lice, sand fleas, mosquitoes)
Invasion of frogs   Infestation of flies

Plague among the livestock   Invasion of locusts
Boils/sores on people and animals   Darkness
Hailstorm   Death of the firstborn

The Bowl Judgments of the Tribulation
(Revelation 16)

Boils/sores on those with the mark   Darkness on the beast's kingdom
   of the beast   Scorching heat
The sea turns to blood   The Euphrates River dries up
The rivers and springs turn to blood   The greatest earthquake in history

12. Recall your answers to question 1. In your opinion, which of these Bowl Judgments would be the most terrifying to live through? Why?

_____

_____

_____

_____

_____

13. Notice the following biblical pattern:
    • God judged the world in the time of Noah.
    • God did not spare the sinful and rebellious cities of Sodom and Gomorrah.
    • Egypt felt the full power of his righteous anger during the days of Moses.
    • Even Israel and Judah were subjected to divine judgment when they violated God's covenant.

    What does this pattern indicate about the certainty of these Seal and Trumpet and Bowl Judgments prophesied for the end times?

_____

_____

_____

_____

_____

"The seven bowl judgments introduced in Revelation 15 and described in chapter 16 are devastating judgments similar to the trumpet judgments, but they are unlike them in that they will affect the whole earth rather than being restricted to one-third of the earth. They will be the final judgments of 'God's wrath' (16:1), apparently given in rapid succession just before the second coming of Christ. These catastrophic judgments are seen as bowls that angels will overturn and pour out on the earth."[4]

John Walvoord

Making the Change

(*Desecration*, pp. 254, 260, 387–88)

Because God is in charge of all things—past, present, and future—it makes perfect sense to get on board with his plans. His will cannot and will not be thwarted. The entire universe is moving toward a divinely ordained conclusion. How foolish for anyone to attempt to do his or her own thing! How arrogant to imagine that we are exempt from God's program for the world! How tragic to miss out on his love and blessings and experience his wrath! Remember the following experiences of those in the Left Behind books who refused to bow to Christ:

CHANG JUMPED UP and turned on the faucet over his sink.
Blood.

_____

"And the blood problem is international."
"Meaning?"
"Intelligence is telling me the waters of the sea are 100 percent blood."
"What sea?"
"Every one. It's crippling us. . . ."

_____

"We have our engineers working around the clock," Carpathia was saying, "on the water issue. All saltwater marine industries are dead, of course. We have lost hundreds of thousands of citizens, who may never be retrieved off the high seas. Vessels can go only so far through a liquid with such a thick, sticky consistency, and the diseases brought by the rotting carcasses of sea creatures may be our most serious health issue ever. Yes, worse than the boils and sores. People only wished they could die from those. The water crisis is again decimating our citizenry."

14. Revelation 16:21 shows the response of many Tribulation survivors, even after witnessing firsthand the terrible series of Seal, Trumpet, and Bowl Judgments. Even with a ringside seat to events that show unmistakably God's holiness, power, and justice, they will curse God, blaming him for their troubles. What does this tell you about the heart of the unrepentant?

_____

_____

_____

_____

_____

"Considering together the Rapture, the four horsemen of the Apocalypse, the many judgments of God, and the martyrdom of the saints during the second half of the Tribulation, it is unlikely that half a billion people will still be living on the planet when Jesus Christ returns. Probably billions will die of the plagues. Others will die from wars, earthquakes, changes in nature, and the other judgments of God. Unsanitary conditions will be everywhere during that time, doubtlessly exacerbating the many infectious diseases that already will be out of control." [5]

Tim LaHaye and Jerry B. Jenkins

15. What does it mean for a person to "harden his/her heart"? (See Exodus 8:15; Psalm 95:8; Daniel 5:20; Ephesians 4:18.)

_____

_____

_____

_____

16. Is your heart soft toward God? Are you willing to listen to him? Are you ready to do anything and everything he says? Take some time to reflect on these questions.

_____

_____

_____

_____

_____

To Ponder

"Sin has a petrifying effect and the heart of the person who continually chooses to sin becomes hardened and paralyzed to spiritual truth, utterly insensitive to the things of God. . . . And when men continually persist in following their own way, they will also eventually be confirmed in their choice by the God of heaven. . . . This is the unspeakable tragedy of unbelief, the tragedy of a person who makes himself his own god." [6]

John MacArthur

Pursuing the Truth

17. For centuries Christians have been saying that Jesus was coming back "soon." How can a modern day believer avoid becoming complacent about the return of Christ?

_____

_____

_____

_____

_____

18. If supernatural miracles can't convince some people of the reality of God and the truth of his Word (and obviously they *can't*—see the experience of Moses, people's response to Christ himself, as well as these passages we've been studying in Revelation), then what *can*? How does your strategy for reaching people with the gospel need to change in order to take this fact into account?

_____

_____

_____

_____

_____

19. Why is it important, as some older Christians have said, to "talk to God about men, before you talk to men about God"?

_____

_____

_____

_____

_____

20. Is it intolerant and judgmental to warn people about the coming wrath of God? Why or why not?

_____

_____

_____

_____

_____

21. How can a Christian warn others of coming judgment without coming across as being judgmental?

_____

_____

_____

_____

_____

Lesson in Review . . .

- Following the Rapture of the church, Antichrist will sign a peace treaty with Israel, officially beginning the Tribulation.
- This seven-year period will be marked by three different series of judgments.
- The final seven judgments are called the Bowl Judgments and will feature the wrath of God poured out upon the earth.
- Despite these clear demonstrations of the holiness and terrible power of God, many will still not turn from their sin.

LEFT

BEHIND

The Judgments

Lesson 6
The Great White Throne

1. Have you had any of the following experiences in your life?
    - being audited by the IRS
    - being sent to the principal's office
    - having to go before a professional accrediting/review board
    - having to give an oral defense of a dissertation or thesis
    - being stopped by police for speeding
    - having to appear in court to defend yourself
    - sitting through a tough job performance review

    If you answered yes to any of these questions, briefly describe one experience of being held accountable—how you felt, what eventually happened, etc.

    _____

    _____

    _____

    _____

2. Imagine having *all* your secrets, thoughts, conversations, and actions replayed on a big screen for all the world to see. How would you respond?

    _____

    _____

    _____

    _____

Unfolding the Story

(*The Remnant,* pp. 230–33)

The Left Behind books give us a fictional look at life on earth following the end-times disappearance of millions of Christians in the event called the Rapture. The twelve books focus primarily on the events of the seven-year Tribulation period, leading up to the millennial reign of Christ. They don't explicitly attempt to describe events beyond that.

Even so, some of the characters from the series speak important words that have bearing on the subject of today's lesson.

"WE FIND OURSELVES ENDURING the worst period in human history. Sixteen of the prophesied judgments of God have already rained down upon the earth, each worse than the last, with five yet to go. The Antichrist has been revealed, as has the False Prophet. That is why Messiah referred to this period as the Tribulation, and the second half of it—in which we now find ourselves—as the Great Tribulation.

"How can I say this judging, avenging God is loving and merciful? Remember that during this period he is working in people to get them to make a decision. Why? The Millennium is coming. When Jesus makes his final glorious appearing, he will come in power and great glory. He will set up his kingdom exclusively for those who have made the right decision. That decision? To call on the name of the Lord.

"Does that sound exclusivistic? Understand this: The Bible makes clear that the will of God is that all men be saved. Second Peter 3:9 says, 'The Lord is not slack concerning his promise, . . . but is long-suffering toward us, not willing that any should perish but that all should come to repentance.'

"God promised in Joel 2 that he would 'show wonders in the heavens and in the earth: blood and fire and pillars of smoke. The sun shall be turned into darkness, and the moon into blood, before the coming of the great and awesome day of the Lord. And it shall come to pass that whoever calls on the name of the Lord shall be saved. For in Mount Zion and in Jerusalem there shall be deliverance, as the Lord has said, among the remnant whom the Lord calls.'

"Dear people, you are that remnant! Do you see what God is saying? He is still calling men to faith in Christ. He has raised up 144,000 evangelists, from the twelve tribes, to plead with men and women all over the world to decide for Christ. Who but a loving, gracious, merciful, long-suffering God could plan in advance that during this time of chaos he would send so many out in power to preach his message? . . .

"Whom will you serve? Will you obey the ruler of this world, or will you call on the name of the Lord?

"God has done all these great and mighty things because he wants to save mankind. Many will still rebel, even here, even after all they have seen and experienced. Do not let it be you, my friend. Our God is merciful. Our God is gracious. He is long-suffering and wants all to be saved.

"If you agree that God is using the period we now live in to get people ready for the millennial kingdom and for eternity, what will you do with your life? Turn it over to Messiah. Worship Jesus, the Christ. Receive him as the one and only Lamb of God that takes away the sins of the world. Receive him into your life and then live in obedience to him. He wants you. And a God who will go to such lengths to save to the uttermost anyone who will call on him is one worth trusting. Will you trust a God like that? Can you love a God like that? . . .

"The time is short," Tsion cried out, "and salvation is a personal decision. Admit to God that you are a sinner. Acknowledge that you cannot save yourself. Throw yourself on the mercy of God and receive the gift of his Son, who died on the cross for your sin. Receive him and thank him for the gift of your salvation."

3. How would you describe Dr. Tsion Ben-Judah's tone in this address?

_____

_____

_____

_____

_____

_____

_____

4. What do his words suggest about the character of God?

_____

_____

_____

_____

_____

_____

Back to Reality

It is sobering to ponder, but the day *is* coming when everyone who has ever lived will have to stand before God. Believers will appear before the judgment seat of Christ (1 Corinthians 3:10–15; 2 Corinthians 5:10). Unbelievers, on the other hand, will give an account at the Great White Throne Judgment (Revelation 20:11–15).

5. When you think about these certain events, what concerns come to mind?

    _____

    _____

    _____

    _____

    _____

    _____

    _____

6. What would you say to critics who charge that Bible studies like this one are wrong, because "you're just trying to scare people into believing in Jesus"?

    _____

    _____

    _____

    _____

    _____

    _____

    _____

7. Many people say they are pretty sure they'll go to heaven after they die. "After all," they often reason, "I've lived a pretty good life, compared to most other people." What's wrong with this kind of logic?

    _____

    _____

    _____

    _____

_____

_____

_____

"The Great White Throne will be unlike any courtroom we have seen because it will have a Judge but no jury, a prosecutor but no defense attorney, and a sentence but no appeal. None of those things will exist in this courtroom because Christ will judge the unbelieving world with absolute justice. Nothing will be missed or overlooked as unsaved people from throughout history appear before Christ in the final judgment of the ages." [1]

Tony Evans

Understanding the Word

John, the writer of the book of Revelation, places the Great White Throne Judgment chronologically just after the Millennium (Christ's thousand-year rule on the earth) and Satan's final rebellion (see Revelation 20). Here is how the Spirit of God moved him to describe the scene:

> *And I saw a great white throne, and I saw the one who was sitting on it. The earth and sky fled from his presence, but they found no place to hide. I saw the dead, both great and small, standing before God's throne. And the books were opened, including the Book of Life. And the dead were judged according to the things written in the books, according to what they had done. The sea gave up the dead in it, and death and the grave gave up the dead in them. They were all judged according to their deeds. And death and the grave were thrown into the lake of fire. This is the second death—the lake of fire. And anyone whose name was not found recorded in the Book of Life was thrown into the lake of fire.* (Revelation 20:11–15)

8. On what basis are people judged at the great white throne?

_____

_____

_____

_____

_____

_____

_____

_____

_____

9. In what way will this judgment take away any excuses people might have?

_____

_____

_____

_____

_____

_____

_____

_____

"Many unbelievers may agree that they are sinners, but they think they aren't all that bad by their standards. They think their sin isn't that big of a deal, and it will be outweighed by the good things they have done. But at the judgment, their sins will be displayed against the perfect holiness of God, and suddenly it will be a very big deal. Most unbelievers will never understand the holiness and perfect justice of God until they see it at the judgment." [2]

Tony Evans

10. Who will be the judge on the throne at this awesome occasion? (Hint: see John 5:22, 27 and Acts 17:31.)

_____

_____

_____

_____

_____

_____

_____

Consider two additional passages that the apostle Paul wrote to Christians living in Corinth:

For no one can lay any other foundation than the one we already have—Jesus Christ. Now anyone who builds on that foundation may use gold, silver, jewels, wood, hay, or straw. But there is going to come a time of testing at the judgment day to see what kind of work each builder has done. Everyone's work will be put through the fire to see whether or not it keeps its value. If the work survives the fire, that builder will receive a reward. But if the work is burned up, the builder will suffer great loss. The builders themselves will be saved, but like someone escaping through a wall of flames. (1 Corinthians 3:11–15)

For we must all stand before Christ to be judged. We will each receive whatever we deserve for the good or evil we have done in our bodies. (2 Corinthians 5:10)

11. How does this judgment day differ from the Great White Throne Judgment? How is it similar?

_____

_____

_____

_____

_____

_____

_____

_____

12. Will believers in Jesus have to stand before the great white throne? On what basis are Christians judged before Christ?

_____

_____

_____

_____

_____

_____

_____

"Revelation 20:12 identifies those who will be judged at the Great White Throne. . . . It is significant to note that these are 'the dead'—dead in trespasses and sins because of the rejection of Jesus Christ, and resurrected in order to appear at this judgment. . . .

"Many people hold to the common misconception that at judgment, God will compare their good deeds with their bad ones, and if the good deeds outweigh the bad, then they will make it to heaven. But good works, no matter how many, cannot help us (Titus 3:5). It all comes down to whether we accept or reject Jesus Christ." [3]

Tim LaHaye and Thomas Ice

Finding the Connection

If anything is clear about the topic of judgment, it is that our choices matter greatly. In fact, our decisions in this life have eternal ramifications!

Consider that God has, as it were, a library of very detailed books. One set of these books contains a complete record of every person's deeds (Revelation 20:12). Remember these statements from the lips of Jesus?

For everything that is hidden or secret will eventually be brought to light and made plain to all. (Luke 8:17)

Whatever you have said in the dark will be heard in the light, and what you have whispered behind closed doors will be shouted from the housetops for all to hear! (Luke 12:3)

In other words, God keeps exhaustive, impeccable records. Consequently, the "defendants" at the Great White Throne Judgment will be without any sort of defense. They will have no case, no justification whatsover. Having pridefully and foolishly refused Christ's lavish offer of full forgiveness and life that never ends, they will be accused and rightfully convicted by their own evil thoughts and actions. Here is the clear evidence that all who are in hell choose their own destiny. As C. S. Lewis observed, there are only two kinds of people in the world. The first kind say to God, "Thy will be done." The second kind refuse to submit, to whom God finally says, "All right, you may have your wish."

13. Immediately following this final judgment, God unveils the new heaven and new earth (Revelation 21:1). What does this sequence of events suggest about God? About sin and purity?

_____
_____
_____
_____
_____
_____
_____

14. What kind of world would we have if lawbreakers were never called to account? What kind of universe would this be if God did not judge evil?

_____
_____
_____
_____
_____
_____
_____
_____

15. Given the unavoidability of God's judgment, how would you approach a friend with your concern that he or she might be "running out of time to repent"?

_____
_____
_____
_____
_____
_____
_____

Making the Change

(*The Mark,* pp. 146–48)

In book eight of the Left Behind series, Dr. Tsion Ben-Judah prepares a message of encouragement and warning. God is a God of lavish love and mercy *and* a God of severe holiness and justice. Both expressions are true. If we do not wrestle with and embrace both realities, we do not have an accurate understanding of God. Tsion's words are appropriate for this study:

> WE ARE ENTERING INTO THE BLOODIEST season in the history of the world. Those who take the mark of the beast will suffer affliction at the hand of God. Those who refuse it will be martyred for his blessed cause. Never has the choice been so stark, so plain.
>
> God himself gave name to this three-and-a-half-year period. Matthew 24:21–22 records Jesus saying, "For then there will be a great tribulation, such as has not been since the beginning of the world until this time, no, nor ever shall be. And unless those days were shortened, no flesh would be saved; but for the elect's [that's you and me, believer] sake those days will be shortened."
>
> In all God's dealings with mankind, this is the shortest period on record, and yet more Scripture is devoted to it than any other period except the life of Christ. While the Hebrew prophets referred to this as a time of "vengeance of our God" for the slaughter of the prophets and saints over the centuries, it is also a time of mercy. God goes to extreme measures to compress the decision-making time for men and women before the coming of Christ to set up his earthly kingdom.
>
> Despite that this is clearly the most awful time in history, I still say it is also a merciful act of God to give as many souls as possible an opportunity to put their faith in Christ. Oh, people, we are the army of God with a massive job to do in a short time. May we do it with willingness and eagerness, and the courage that comes only from him. There are countless lost souls in need of saving, and we have the truth.
>
> It may be hard to recognize God's mercy when his wrath is also intensifying. Woe

to those who believe the lie that God is only "love." Yes, he is love. And his gift of Jesus as the sacrifice for our sin is the greatest evidence of this. But the Bible also says God is "holy, holy, holy." He is righteous and a God of justice, and it is not in his nature to allow sin to go unpunished or unpaid for.

16. In light of what is to come, how does Tsion challenge his fellow believers?

_____

_____

_____

_____

_____

_____

_____

17. In one place, a Left Behind character argues that people can either follow God and suffer now for the short term, or reject God and suffer eternally. What do you think of this stark choice?

_____

_____

_____

_____

_____

_____

18. Do you agree with Tsion, that it is hard to "recognize God's mercy when his wrath is also intensifying"? Why is it hard to reconcile these aspects?

_____

_____

_____

_____

_____

"I have often heard the ungodly boast that on the Day of Judgment they would demand that God justify Himself for the wrongs of the world, but this is sheer, wicked fantasy. It will never happen. If beloved Daniel collapsed in fear and utter weakness when he saw a vision of the heavenly being (and those with him did not even see it but still hid themselves in terror, Daniel 10:4–8); if the apostle John fell like a dead man when he saw a vision of the resurrected Christ (Revelation 1:10–17); if righteous Job, who had been demanding an audience with God, would say, 'I have heard of You by the hearing of the ear, but now my eye sees You. Therefore I abhor myself, and repent in dust and ashes' when his demand was met (Job 42:5–6)—then what madness is this for the wicked to imagine they will justify themselves before God on the day they stand before Him at the great white throne!" [5]

Tim LaHaye and Jerry B. Jenkins

Pursuing the Truth

19. What do the following Bible passages tell you about the thoroughness of the Lord's judgment?

_____

_____

_____

_____

_____

_____

_____

_____

God will judge us for everything we do, including every secret thing, whether good or bad. (Ecclesiastes 12:14)

For there is going to come a day of judgment when God, the just judge of all the world, will judge all people according to what they have done. He will give eternal life to those who persist in doing what is good, seeking after the glory and honor and immortality that God offers. But he will pour out his anger and wrath on those who live for themselves, who refuse to obey the truth and practice evil deeds. (Romans 2:5–8)

20. Read Revelation 20:11–15 again. What is the stated destiny of those whose names are not written in the Book of Life?

_____

_____

_____

_____

_____

_____

21. How is the "lake of fire" described in the following verses?
Matthew 25:41

_____

Mark 9:43

_____

Revelation 21:8

_____

22. Read Philippians 2:10–11. In the end, what will be the universal response to Jesus Christ, Lord and Judge of all the earth?

_____

_____

_____

_____

_____

Wise Words to Consider

"The fact of eternal punishment of the lost should motivate Christians to do all they can to lead people to Christ before it is too late. While heaven will be a wonderful reunion of those who are saved, there will be no such fellowship in hell. . . . Apart from faith in Christ there is no mercy or grace. In His holiness and righteousness God has no alternative but to punish those, whether angels or people, who continue to sin against Him."[6]

John Walvoord

23. As you ponder all the terrible judgments to come, think about the people in your life who have not yet acknowledged Christ as Savior. What specific action steps can you take this week to share the good news of Christ with them?

_____

_____

_____

_____

_____

_____

_____

Lesson in Review . . .

- Following the Millennium and one last revolt by Satan (Revelation 20:7–10), the unbelieving dead will face a terrible and final judgment.
- This event is commonly known as the Great White Throne Judgment, and Christ himself will oversee the proceedings.
- The Lord's perfect justice and mercy will be evident to all, as will the utter sinfulness and rebelliousness of those who rejected Christ.
- Christians do not have to fear this judgment; it is for unbelievers only.
- The coming judgment should motivate believers to take the message of Christ to the nations.

Endnotes

Lesson 1: Here Comes the Judge!

1. *Life Application New Testament Commentary*, ed. Philip W. Comfort and Dan Lins (Wheaton: Tyndale House, 2001), 582.
2. Charles Ryrie, *The Ryrie Study Bible* (Chicago: Moody, 1976), 1703.
3. Howard Hendricks, *Living by the Book* (Chicago: Moody, 1991), 231.
4. Tim LaHaye and Jerry B. Jenkins, *Are We Living in the End Times?* (Wheaton: Tyndale House, 1999), 155–56.
5. Ibid., 157–58.
6. Hendricks, *Living by the Book,* 200.

Lesson 2: The Day of the Lord

1. Charles Ryrie, *The Ryrie Study Bible* (Chicago: Moody, 1976), 1809.
2. Mark Bailey quoted in *Prophecy in Light of Today,* ed. Charles H. Dyer (Chicago: Moody, 2002), 93–94.
3. Charles Ryrie, *Basic Theology* (Chicago: Moody, 1986), 464.
4. Bailey in *Prophecy in Light of Today,* 96.
5. Tony Evans, *The Best Is Yet to Come* (Chicago: Moody, 2000), 190.
6. Tim LaHaye and Jerry B. Jenkins, *Are We Living in the End Times?* (Wheaton: Tyndale House, 1999), 151.

Lesson 3: Breaking the Seals

1. Charles Ryrie, *Everyman's Bible Commentary: Revelation* (Chicago: Moody, 1968), 46.
2. Tim LaHaye and Jerry B. Jenkins, *Are We Living in the End Times?* (Wheaton: Tyndale House, 1999), 185.
3. Larry Mercer quoted in *Prophecy in Light of Today,* ed. Charles H. Dyer (Chicago: Moody, 2002), 122.

Lesson 4: Blowing the Trumpets

1. Tim LaHaye and Jerry B. Jenkins, *Are We Living in the End Times?* (Wheaton: Tyndale House, 1999), 187.
2. Ibid., 187–88.

3. Charles Ryrie, *The Ryrie Study Bible* (Chicago: Moody, 1976), 1905.

4. LaHaye and Jenkins, *Are We Living in the End Times?* 189–90.

5. Charles Ryrie, *Everyman's Bible Commentary: Revelation* (Chicago: Moody, 1996), 74.

6. John Walvoord, *End Times: Understanding Today's World Events in Biblical Prophecy* (Nashville: Word, 1998), 220.

7. Tony Evans, *The Best Is Yet to Come* (Chicago: Moody, 2000), 197.

Lesson 5: The Overturned Bowls

1. Tim LaHaye and Thomas Ice, *Charting the End Times* (Eugene, Ore.: Harvest House, 2001), 61–62.

2. Charles Ryrie, *Basic Theology* (Chicago: Moody, 1986), 476.

3. Tim LaHaye and Jerry B. Jenkins, *Are We Living in the End Times?* (Wheaton: Tyndale House, 1999), 207–8.

4. John Walvoord, *End Times: Understanding Today's World Events in Biblical Prophecy* (Nashville: Word, 1998), 129.

5. LaHaye and Jenkins, *Are We Living in the End Times?* 179.

6. John MacArthur, *Ephesians* (Chicago: Moody, 1986), 169–70.

Lesson 6: The Great White Throne

1. Tony Evans, *The Best Is Yet to Come* (Chicago: Moody, 2000), 241.

2. Ibid., 243.

3. Tim LaHaye and Thomas Ice, *Charting the End Times* (Eugene, Ore.: Harvest House, 2001), 73–74.

4. Evans, *The Best Is Yet to Come*, 240.

5. Tim LaHaye and Jerry B. Jenkins, *Are We Living in the End Times?* (Wheaton: Tyndale House, 1999), 251–52.

6. John Walvoord, *End Times: Understanding Today's World Events in Biblical Prophecy* (Nashville: Word, 1998), 184.